ENDORSEMENTS

Greg Mohr has written yet a _____ _ng in *the Supernatural* could not be mo_____ only do churches today have great need for the power and the presence of God in their midst, but believers need wisdom, discernment, and common sense in order to operate in the Holy Spirit's gifts effectively. Greg provides great biblical and practical instruction in both areas. The gifts of the Holy Spirit are powerful, wonderful tools to be used for the edification of others, not toys to be played with for one's own pleasure. Thank you, Greg, for sharing vital insights that will help us maximize the help that we receive from the Helper!

TONY COOKE
Founder and President of Tony Cooke Ministries
Broken Arrow, Oklahoma

In a day when the gifts of the Spirit are either overlooked or misused, this book by Greg Mohr is a tremendous gift to the body of Christ. Greg's sound biblical teaching on this vital subject is the result of a lifetime of fruitful ministry and is sure to be a blessing to those who want to flow in the supernatural. I highly recommend this book to anyone who wants a scriptural understanding of the gifts of the Holy Spirit.

GREG FRITZ
Founder and President of Greg Fritz Ministries
Tulsa, Oklahoma

Revival begins with a returning to the Holy Spirit, His power for miracles, and supernatural assistance to fulfill the Great Commission. Then His gifts return to our lives and our local churches. After a long drought of the Spirit's power in our churches, there is a return today. My friend and fellow teacher, Greg Mohr, is helping to lead that return with his book *Flowing in the Supernatural*. It will be a blessing to your life and church.

PASTOR BOB YANDIAN
Founder and President of Bob Yandian Ministries
Tulsa, Oklahoma

In my opinion, the first chapter really describes Greg's heart and reason for writing this book. The supernatural power and gifts of the Holy Spirit are not only available to the church today, they are absolutely the mark of the last-days church. The pendulum is swinging back from the pop culture church to the authentic, biblical church of Jesus Christ. Application of these truths to your life and ministry will return you to a sound spiritual foundation and prepare you for the appearance of Christ in the heavens.

PASTOR HAPPY CALDWELL
Founder and President of VTN Television Network
and Happy Caldwell Ministries
Little Rock, Arkansas

Many people have experience but lack the anointing. Others have the anointing but limited experience in the supernatural. Greg Mohr is the epitome of anointed experience. Greg is a man of great faith and grace I have known since 1990. His practical, Word-based ministry is both powerful and refreshing.

Greg Mohr's new book, *Flowing in the Supernatural*, is greatly needed in the Body of Christ today. A born-again, Spirit-filled believer's DNA is the supernatural power of the Holy Spirit. This book will guide you in flowing in the supernatural power of God. It will help you understand the balance of the supernatural and its practical application in ministry.

I wholeheartedly recommend Greg Mohr's book, *Flowing in the Supernatural*, to everyone who desires to be used of God in these last days.

Dr. Bob Nichols
Pastor, Calvary Cathedral International
Fort Worth, Texas

Greg Mohr's book *Flowing in the Supernatural* gives us very simple and practical keys for the book of Acts to become the way of life for every believer. Greg shows us how the supernatural can become normal and how each of us can operate in the Holy Spirit's gifts with confidence without being weird and flaky.

James Brown
Network Broadcaster, CBS Sports and News
Bethesda, Maryland

Finally, a balance between the supernatural power of God and divine order without cancelling one another out. We can have both that complement one another. A false balance is an abomination, but God delights in a just weight. Thank you, Greg, for helping the body of Christ bring that balance to their lives and churches.

Pastor Duane Sheriff
Senior Pastor of Victory Life Church
Durant, Oklahoma

I'm so excited that Greg has written this abundantly practical book to resource us with wisdom, faith, courage, common sense, and encouragement to flow in a supernatural lifestyle! Read this and grow!

Sarah Bowling
Founder of Saving Moses Ministry
and Pastor of Encounter Church
Denver, Colorado

Pastor Greg Mohr has hit a home run in his book *Flowing in the Supernatural*. He effectively addresses the error we have seen in the Body of Christ regarding the supernatural that has caused so many to avoid the subject altogether. Then he scripturally brings us back to what the Lord has intended from the beginning, to be a church that the gates of hell cannot prevail against. I believe this is a now word for all believers to begin to *covet earnestly* the greater manifestations of the gifts of the Spirit. Thank you Pastor Greg for being obedient to the Lord in writing this book.

MARK COWART
Senior Pastor, Church For All Nations
Colorado Springs, Colorado

FLOWING *in the* SUPERNATURAL

*Your Guide to Understanding & Operating
in the Gifts of the Holy Spirit*

GREG MOHR

DESTINY IMAGE® PUBLISHERS, INC.

P.O. Box 310, Shippensburg, PA 17257-0310

"Promoting Inspired Lives."

This book and all other Destiny Image and Destiny Image Fiction books are available at Christian bookstores and distributors worldwide.

Cover design by Eileen Rockwell
Interior design by Terry Clifton

For more information on foreign distributors, call 717-532-3040.

Reach us on the Internet: www.destinyimage.com.

ISBN 13 TP: 978-0-7684-4663-0
ISBN 13 eBook: 978-0-7684-4664-7
ISBN 13 HC: 978-0-7684-4666-1
ISBN 13 LP: 978-0-7684-4665-4

For Worldwide Distribution, Printed in the U.S.A.
1 2 3 4 5 6 7 8 / 23 22 21 20 19

DEDICATION

I WANT TO DEDICATE THIS BOOK TO SIX MEN WHO HAVE BEEN MEN-
tors to me over the past forty years of ministry. Each one has taught
and modeled the operation of the gifts of the Spirit and the move of
the Spirit in different ways. Their ministry and influence in my life
has been a great training ground I am now able to pass on to you.

First, is Kenneth Hagin, Sr. who taught me about the gifts,
defined them, and gave practical examples of their use both in the
Bible and through his ministry.

Second, is John Osteen who was an excellent example for me of
a pastor of a large church who allowed the gifts to operate in their
church services. He also modeled how the move of the Spirit and
Biblical order can function together.

Third, is Ron Smith who came to our church each year as a
guest minister for twenty-four years. Ron functioned in the office
of the prophet and was a modern-day prophet to our church. He
demonstrated the operation of the gifts in powerful and practical
ways. He also challenged me and my church leaders to move in the
gifts with confidence.

Next, is Jack Hayford who I have called the Apostle of Balance.
He taught me how to teach on the baptism of the Holy Spirit and
the gifts of the Spirit, and model them in practical ways that make
them attractive to people rather than offensive.

Next is my pastor, Bob Nichols. I have never met a pastor
or minister who has as much passion for and has provided such
long-lasting leadership for the move of the Spirit in the local church.

He has been available to me to answer many questions I have had regarding "pastoring" the move of God. He has modeled a radical balance between the Word and the Spirit.

Finally, is Andrew Wommack who is one of the premier teachers of the Word of God in the body of Christ who teaches the baptism in the Spirit and gifts of the Spirit unashamedly. He also operates in the gifts with ease and confidence and celebrates the variety of different ministries who operate the gifts in different ways than he does.

CONTENTS

FOREWORD

Honestly, Greg Mohr is my favorite guest on my television program, *Today With Marilyn and Sarah*! He presents faith in a very simple and applicable way. He reveals that faith is simple and applicable to all! Sometimes people mistakenly believe that the gifts of the Spirit are mysterious and not available to everyone!

Open your eyes to the truth that these gifts are available to all believers! He beautifully reveals in his book *Flowing in the Supernatural* the environment they operate in!

Do you have a hunger for the supernatural? This book will bring a spiritual explosion in your life!

Get ready for the supernatural!

Marilyn Hickey
Founder and President of Marilyn Hickey Ministries
and *Marilyn and Sarah* television broadcast
Denver, Colorado

INTRODUCTION

THE BAPTISM OF THE HOLY SPIRIT AND THE GIFTS THAT HE brings to the church are indispensable for victory in the Christian life. Sadly, there are many Christians today who are just like the people in Acts 19 who said, "We have not even heard if there be a Holy Spirit" (see Acts 19:2 KJV).

Then there are others who have heard of the Holy Spirit but they've seen so many weird things that were blamed on the Holy Spirit that at the very least they are confused and at the worst, many have run the other direction because of the abuses.

Paul told us in First Corinthians 12:1 that he doesn't want us ignorant concerning the gifts of the Holy Spirit and their proper operation, and yet this is one of the areas where ignorance persists in the body of Christ. It is time, it is past time, for a clear presentation

of the truth in this regard. I believe Greg Mohr's book is an answer for that.

I've known Greg and Janice Mohr for three decades. I ministered in their church in Decatur, Texas, many times and was very impressed with what the Lord was doing there. The fingerprints of the Lord were all over that ministry. It was not strange or unusual to have the gifts of the Holy Spirit in operation in their services and yet it was always done decently and in order.

I've now been blessed to have Greg serve in our ministry for the past seven years and direct our main campus of Charis Bible College in Woodland Park, Colorado, for the last three years. He has brought that same sensitivity to the Holy Spirit to our ministry and it is impacting our students all over the world.

Jesus told His disciples not to go anywhere or tell anyone what had happened until they received the power of God through the baptism of the Holy Spirit. Think of that! They had the greatest news the world will ever hear and yet the Lord told them not to share it until they received the power of the Holy Spirit. The Lord didn't want them ministering out of their own ability. Neither should we.

Today the modern church has to a large degree substituted technology and style for the Holy Spirit. The churches that do believe in the ministry of the Holy Spirit have pretty much relegated Him to the back room so no one will be offended at His presence. That's not right. On the day of Pentecost the Holy Spirit came in a very open and spectacular way and the result was that three thousand people got saved. We need the open demonstration of the Holy Spirit in our churches today.

But sadly, when churches do permit the gifts of the Holy Spirit to operate, it is often abused. That leads to many problems which eventually leads to them backing away from that freedom. It doesn't have to be that way.

The Scriptures teach that the elders are supposed to judge and give direction in the services. Sure, there will be mistakes made but with the right guidance, the gifts of the Holy Spirit are powerful to the body as a whole and also to the individual who learns to yield and cooperate with Him. We need the Holy Spirit in our services but we also need it done properly.

Praise God, He didn't leave us to figure this out on our own. The Lord gave ample instruction in His Word about how the Holy Spirit operates and how we are to respond. Greg brings out that wisdom through this book and his decades of practical experience in this area.

This book will provide practical instruction for pastors and individuals alike. If you are tired of doing it on your own, if you are hungry to see God's supernatural power demonstrated through you, if you long to see God confirm His word as He did in the early church, then this book is for you.

Get ready to learn and experience a greater degree of God's power working in and through you by the Holy Spirit. You will never be the same.

ANDREW WOMMACK

Chapter 1

THE SUPERNATURAL IS AVAILABLE TO US TODAY

Do you desire to see the supernatural operate through your life? Do you long to see healings, miracles, signs, and wonders occur on a regular basis? Do you want to find and be part of a church that models what we see in the book of Acts? Then this book is for you. It is not an accident the Spirit drew your attention to this book and led you to pick it up and read it. My goal is to help restore the supernatural in the church and to empower individuals to walk in confidence in releasing the gifts of the Spirit in their lives. The supernatural is supposed to be the norm for the church, not the exception.

We don't need to return to the times of the book of Acts but to the principles upon which the early church was founded. That is

the Word, the Spirit, the blood, the cross, His name, His presence and His healing power. We should not settle for anything less than a church operating in the power of God with regular demonstrations of the Spirit that set people free and draw them to the Lord. His church is a supernatural church that is distinct from every other religion and social club. We follow a resurrected Christ who is alive and present to do what He did when He walked the earth.

Slick programs and marketing campaigns are poor substitutes for the presence of God and the power of God! Yet that is what many churches have degraded into today. There is a huge disparity between dead, dry religion and a genuine move of the Spirit birthed by the ministry of the Word, the presence of God, and demonstrations of the Spirit of God. People are looking for the real deal today. They are hungry for the supernatural power of God and the Word of God.

I haven't always known the true power of God and operated in the supernatural. I wasn't raised in a strong Christian home. My parents were divorced when I was eight years of age. My mom and grandparents would take me occasionally to a denominational church in the city I lived in the Midwest. If I ever heard the message of the gospel taught one time when I attended that church, I don't know it.

Later we moved to Texas and we occasionally attended a Baptist church. This is where I first heard the gospel preached. I didn't receive the Lord during that time because I was too busy trying to impress the girls and I didn't want anyone to know I wasn't saved. When I met my future wife, I started attending the large Methodist church she belonged to. After we were married I received the Lord in that Methodist church based on the Word I had heard in the Baptist church I attended seven years before. In each of these three denominational churches I had attended, we rarely observed anything supernatural happening. The only exception to that was those who received salvation in the Baptist church where I first heard the gospel.

A couple of times during my teenage years I attended a Pentecostal church with one of my friends. What I observed there was the appearance of the supernatural, but it did not seem genuine. All the women had their hair up in buns, wore long dresses with long sleeves and no makeup. I guess the point of that was to appear holy so God would move supernaturally through them. Then the preacher would stand up and preach (yell) for an hour. Every time he would say "God," he said it like this, "God-ah." I guess he thought the volume of his preaching and the way he said God would release a greater anointing. Then it seemed like he was manipulating a move of the Spirit in the people by shaming them and "condemning" them to come down to the altar and get their lives right with God.

This didn't look anything closer to the church in the book of Acts than the other three churches in those mainline denominations I attended. After I received the Lord, I would read the four gospels and the book of Acts and ask the Lord, "Where is a church today like what I see in Jesus' ministry and the book of Acts?" During that time, I watched a few TV programs with Kathryn Kuhlman and Oral Roberts where they were ministering the Word and healing the sick. I was really attracted to these ministries. They were seeing many miracles, and people would share their healing testimonies. It was hard to deny this was the real supernatural power of God I had read about in the gospels and the book of Acts. And it was happening again today!

The other thing that attracted me to these two ministries is they both seemed so genuine, sincere, and full of the love of God. I asked the Lord, "How do they perform miracles and see so many people healed and saved in their ministries and crusades? Was there something special about them that caused You to choose them and use them in these ways? Or could it be possible that John 14:12 I had read many times was true and we could all operate in the supernatural power of God?"

> *Most assuredly I say to you, he who believes in Me, the works that I do he will do also; and greater works than these he will do, because I go to My Father* (John 14:12).

I didn't hear the Lord speak anything to me at that time. There was just a strong sense in my heart that the supernatural was still for the church today and available to those who believed what Jesus said in John 14:12. The problem was I did not know any individuals or churches that believed and modeled this. The church we were attending was dead from my perspective. The pastor would preach many times out of the newspaper or the *Reader's Digest*. And I was becoming more and more dissatisfied and seeking the Lord for a genuine demonstration of the supernatural like I saw in the book of Acts.

It is not possible to seek the Lord regarding something He has promised in His Word and it not be fulfilled.

> *Blessed are those who hunger and thirst for righteousness, for they shall be filled* (Matthew 5:6).

At this time my wife and I found a Christian television network that broadcast in our area. It was called the *700 Club*. Pat Robertson and Ben Kinchlow were the hosts. Each program highlighted supernatural testimonies of God's saving, delivering, and healing power in the lives of people. I was drawn and attracted to these TV ministry hosts in the same way I was a few years before to Kathryn Kuhlman and Oral Roberts. There was something genuine and sincere about these men and there was no denying the things I read about in the book of Acts were happening through their ministry.

I could see the love of God in their eyes and feel it coming from their hearts through these broadcasts directly into my heart. Could it be God was answering my prayer by leading me to watch this program? They began to teach about the book of Acts and the things we read there were available for each of us today. Then they taught about the Baptism in the Holy Spirit. They said this was a subsequent experience to salvation and it was essential to operating in the supernatural. They showed us in the Word when the church started, all the disciples were filled with the Spirit and received a new spiritual language—tongues. This gave them power to go out and witness and do the works of Jesus!

> *But you shall receive power when the Holy Spirit has come upon you; and you shall be witnesses to Me in Jerusalem, and in all Judea and Samaria, and to the end of the earth* (Acts 1:8).

> *And they were all filled with the Holy Spirit and began to speak with other tongues, as the Spirit gave them utterance* (Acts 2:4).

They said that receiving the Baptism in the Spirit was the key to releasing the supernatural in our lives and seeing the same things we read about in the book of Acts manifest today. I had never heard about this in any of the churches I had attended. I am sure that is why we weren't seeing the supernatural things today as we saw in the book of Acts. Within a few weeks my wife and I were both filled with the Spirit. We also found a Spirit-filled church that taught and believed in the Baptism in the Holy Spirit, the gifts of the Spirit, and the healing power of God. Once we received the Baptism in the

Spirit with the evidence of speaking in other tongues, my wife and I both became much more sensitive to the Holy Spirit and available to release the gifts of the Spirit and minister healing to others.

Filled with the Spirit

This was amazing. None of this happened prior to us being filled with the Spirit. But now we were seeing supernatural things manifest in and through our lives on a regular basis. We learned how to have a personal relationship with the Holy Spirit as we prayed in the Spirit, listened to and were led by the Spirit, and remained dependent upon the Spirit each day. We actually began living out the book of Acts in our lives. Praise God, He answered our prayer and desire to flow in the supernatural. And He will do the same for you!

For more than four decades now, my wife and I have experienced signs, wonders, and miracles. The supernatural has operated freely through our lives. We have witnessed the blind see, the deaf hear, and the lame walk. I was healed of cancer in 1977. Our son, Michael, was healed of a serious muscular, arthritic condition the following year. Our daughter-in-law, Jessica, received a miracle healing of the supernatural removal of scar tissue from her internal organs that allowed her to give us three additional grandchildren! And our granddaughter, Joelle, received a miracle healing from clubbed feet in her mother's womb.

We have seen scores of people healed through our church, ministry, and through previous books I have written. (See gregmohr.com for more information on these books.) We have also witnessed literally thousands of normal, average, everyday believers and church members heal the sick, perform miracles, and move in the supernatural. The book of Acts is the only book in the New Testament that is not complete. It is one of the few books that doesn't have an "Amen" at the end of it. We are living now in Acts chapter 29! Jesus is the same yesterday, today, and forever. He is still doing through His church what He did when He walked the earth.

> *So Jesus said to them again, "Peace to you! As the Father has sent Me, I also send you"* (John 20:21).

Whatever you see Jesus doing in the gospels and the church doing in the book of Acts, He has sent you and me to do. That is a powerful revelation. We are His body on the earth today—His arms and hands extended to a lost and hurting world. Will you go for Him? This book, *Flowing in the Supernatural,* will help you develop confidence in operating in the gifts and moving in the supernatural. God shows no favorites. If He will do that for us, He will do it for you.

If you have not yet been filled with the Spirit with the evidence of speaking in other tongues, I encourage you to skip over to Chapters 19 and 20 in this book: "The Baptism in the Holy Spirit is the Doorway to the Supernatural" and "The Benefits of Praying in Tongues." Once you receive this precious gift of being filled with the Spirit, your understanding and heart will be much more receptive to the other principles in this book.

I pray that you will be filled with the Spirit, receive the spirit of wisdom and revelation in the knowledge of Jesus, and the eyes of your understanding will be enlightened to know all that is available to you to do His works and move in the supernatural!

Chapter 2

Don't Be Ignorant

Pursuing this quest of learning to flow in the supernatural will cause you to be filled with God's presence, receive fresh revelation of Jesus, and powerful ministry opportunities. You will discover wonderful gifts available to you that you may have only seen or heard of but not yet experienced firsthand. You will also learn how to operate them in confidence and biblical order—the way they were intended to function.

Maybe you are like me and have seen the gifts manifest in a weird or flaky way through some well-intentioned, but zealous Christian sometime in the past. That tempted you to shy away from the gifts for fear you might demonstrate them in a similar way and influence someone in a negative way. There is no need to fear this at all. The purpose of this book is to train you how to operate the gifts in a way God will use to influence others to be drawn closer to Him rather than turn away from Him.

These nine wonderful gifts of the Spirit are just that: gifts from God for us to use to minister His love, mercy, and grace to hurting people. Where do we start in this training? With Paul's instruction to the Corinthian church and the present-day church—you and me—about how to operate in these gifts. He begins this instruction in his first letter to the Corinthian church in chapter 12.

> *Now concerning spiritual gifts, brethren, I do not want you to be ignorant* (1 Corinthians 12:1).

I can certainly identify with this verse. I was so ignorant of this dimension of spiritual life prior to being filled with the Spirit. Even after I was filled with the Spirit there was still so much I was ignorant about. What are the gifts and how do they operate? Which demonstrations are appropriate and biblical and which are not? How could I begin getting involved operating the gifts? This requires good biblical teaching on the subject, modeling by spiritual leaders, and others, and opportunity to interact and ask questions from those who are not ignorant about this important part of our spiritual life. This book addresses many questions I first had about how the gifts of the Spirit and the supernatural can be released in confidence and biblical order through our lives today.

Paul begins his instruction to the church not to remain ignorant about spiritual gifts and the potential of the supernatural power of God operating through us. Please don't allow yourself to be put off or offended by the title of this chapter. It comes directly from the beginning of three chapters in the Word devoted to instructing the church on the subject of this book, *Flowing in the Supernatural.*

The word "gifts" in this verse is italicized in the Bible which means it is not in the original Greek text. The word "spiritual" here refers to things pertaining to the Spirit and the supernatural. This, of course, would include the gifts of the Spirit because they are described later in First Corinthians chapter 12 and instruction is also given how to operate in the vocal gifts in chapter 14.

At the outset of First Corinthians, God tells us He does not want us to be ignorant about the gifts of the Spirit, the supernatural, and things of the Spirit. Yet I don't know a single principle of the New Testament that the present-day church is more ignorant and dysfunctional about. You can visit ten Spirit-filled churches in any city today and you would be hard-pressed to find even one of ten that either promotes or allows any type of demonstration of the Spirit in their Sunday morning service. There is also a similar void in the lack of teaching or giving people opportunity to receive the Baptism in the Holy Spirit or healing.

There is a reason for this. In over forty years of Spirit-filled life and ministry I have observed various churches tolerate abuse of the operation of the gifts and allow an individual's personal liberty to trump love and the best interest of the whole body.

Biblical Guidelines

So many Spirit-filled, Charismatic, and Pentecostal churches who taught about the gifts of the Spirit and allowed these gifts to function in their services failed to establish biblical guidelines for their members to follow. The result was chaos, confusion, and people who were unfamiliar with these precious gifts turned off by the way they were demonstrated.

In order to compensate for this problem many pastors and spiritual leaders have established guidelines that do not allow any expression of the gifts at all. Their desire for church growth and their fear regarding individuals operating the gifts in some weird, fleshly way has caused the pendulum to swing from the ditch of no order and chaos to perfect order—but no sign of the supernatural at all in their services.

There are actually entire movements and networks of churches today whose leaders are personally filled with the Spirit but they refuse to allow any manifestation of the Spirit in their Sunday morning or public services. I have heard some of these leaders justify this decision by sharing their heart to reach the lost. They typically will share how they have observed in their past someone who manifested one of the gifts in a weird, flaky way. They go on to share how this turned off an unbeliever they had brought to church that day to be saved. Therefore, because it is the Lord's heart and theirs to reach the lost, they have made this decision not to allow the operation of the gifts in their primary services so they don't turn off seeking people who come to their church.

They will use Scriptures like the following verse to establish their case:

> *Therefore if the whole church comes together in one place,*
> *and all speak with tongues, and there come in those who*
> *are uninformed or unbelievers, will they not say that you*
> *are out of your mind?* (1 Corinthians 14:23).

I agree with this verse completely, but it does not make the case for allowing no expression of the gifts in the church. If that were true how do you explain verse 39?

> *Wherefore, brethren, covet to prophesy, and forbid not to*
> *speak with tongues* (1 Corinthians 14:39 KJV).

Many of these leaders are not only forbidding the expression of the public gift of tongues but all other expressions of the nine gifts of the Spirit in the name of reaching more lost people for Christ. I cannot relate to this at all. The Holy Spirit is my everything. He is the Spirit of truth who knows all things and will reveal all things to me I need to know. He will also show me things to come. I depend on Him 24/7. I could not function in ministry and remain sane without Him. I know the same thing is true for all of God's people. I refuse to be embarrassed by or ashamed of Him, nor of the demonstrations of His precious gifts to the church!

Now let me make it clear, in each case I have heard a contemporary church leader use this reasoning I don't doubt the good intention of their heart. Nor am I judging them for their decision. Each of us has to stand before God for how we lead the people the Lord has entrusted us with and to follow the vision He has given us for His church. I simply want to challenge the basis for their decision by the clear instruction of God's Word. I used First Corinthians 14:23 that refers to the use of tongues causing confusion in the church. I want you to look at verse 22 with me now:

> *Therefore tongues are for a sign, not to those who believe but to unbelievers; but prophesying is not for unbelievers but for those who believe* (1 Corinthians 14:22).

Wow! This verse declares exactly the opposite view of some of these contemporary church leaders. God says here tongues are for a sign to unbelievers. He didn't say it would run unbelievers off! I have to respectfully disagree with these leaders and agree with the Word of God. Well then what is verse 23 speaking of when Paul says the use of tongues will cause unbelievers to think you are mad or out of your mind?

Edification and Order

When you study chapter 14 of First Corinthians, you find the two primary themes are edification and order. The Corinthian church was one of those churches where the gifts were operating abundantly, but there was also much abuse and confusion. Paul is correcting this by establishing order for the public use of the gifts.

In verses 22 and 23, he is making a distinction between tongues operated in biblical order and tongues operated out of order. In verse 22 he says tongues operated in order—one person giving a message in tongues and one person interpreting that message in public—is a supernatural sign to an unbeliever. This means when a public expression of tongues and interpretation of tongues is demonstrated in the way God intended, it will draw people to the Lord, not turn them away.

In verse 23, Paul is describing a public demonstration of tongues that is out of order and will cause unbelievers to think you are weird or crazy. If the whole church comes together and *all* speak with tongues out loud *at the same time* it will create confusion among unbelievers or unlearned believers. These two verses are describing two distinct and different public demonstrations of the gift of tongues. One is in biblical order, verse 22, and the other is not, verse 23. So many leaders and churches have gone the "seeker sensitive" route of either forbidding the gifts or putting them in a closet because they do not understand this difference.

The purpose of this book is to encourage the restoration of the supernatural to the church and help establish biblical order for the use of the gifts. In First Corinthians 12:1, the Lord tells us He doesn't want us to be ignorant of spiritual gifts. Then He spends three chapters—12, 13, and 14—"de-ignorantizing" us. Pardon my liberty with the English language. This is a new word I made up as another way to describe the process of informing us. Much of this book will unpack and share practical application of the principles shared in these three chapters of the Word.

The gifts of the Spirit are weapons available to us when we have done all we know to do from the Word and we have not yet received a breakthrough. Or…when we have shared all we know to share with someone who needs help and the person didn't receive it, understand it, or experience any change. Or…when someone needs healing, a miracle, a financial or relational breakthrough, and the person doesn't have the time or emotional or mental capacity to get the revelation they need from the Word first.

Revelation and Faith

Let me make something very clear: it is always better to receive healing, financial blessing, or whatever we need by revelation of the Word and our faith in the Word. Whatever you and I receive by revelation and faith in God's Word, we will not lose later. But the truth is, each of us only knows in part. None of us has revelation on every part of the Word. I am constantly searching out the Word, meditating on it and receiving new revelation every day that sets me "freer" than I was the day before. But there will be times in our lives when our *knowledge* of the Word, not the Word, is not enough to provide us the victory we need because we only know in part.

Whenever I experience this, I focus on two things. First, I spend more time in the Word to receive the revelation I need to put me over. Second, I realize I have the gifts of the Spirit available to me and consciously yield to Him. After all, is He not the Spirit of Truth who will guide you and me into all truth and teach us the truth we need whenever we "hit the wall" and cannot see our way over, around, or through a challenging situation?

There have been numerous times in my walk with the Lord when I faced a situation either my knowledge of the Word or experience was not enough to help me. As I would pray in the Spirit, invariably I would receive a word of knowledge, a word of wisdom, or a Scripture verse that was exactly what I needed. Thank God for the gifts of the Holy Spirit!

Several years ago, my wife and I invited two couples to our home for a meal and fellowship. We were all Bible college students and met for fellowship, encouragement, and connection. One of the couples, Hal and Bobbie, was from Ohio. After the meal, they were sharing with Janice and me and the other couple about the problems they had been having since attending Bible college. They were behind on their tuition payments because a financial commitment back home had not yet come through. They were a blended family and hadn't heard from Bobbie's twenty-year-old daughter in two years.

Then their five-year-old son had been suffering from severe ear infections that kept him up at night. Up to that point the doctors had not been able to find anything to relieve his pain or help him overcome these infections. The other couple and Janice and I shared an abundance of Scriptures with them in an attempt to build their faith and encourage them. We also prayed for them, but the reality was they left more discouraged than when they arrived. We shared all the Word we knew as well as our personal testimonies with them and yet they seemed worse off.

After they left, Janice and I spent time praying in the Spirit together for Hal and Bobbie. While we were praying for them I had three visions. The first was a large metal anvil or wedge that was in Bobbie's arm creating a large, open wound. The second was a little ghost-like creature that looked like Casper the friendly ghost carrying an open medical bag filled with various vials of viruses and bacterial infections. The third was a picture of Hal with handcuffs and chains on his hands.

Instantly I knew by the Spirit these were three different evil spirits that had been assigned to them and were attacking them. I knew the anvil and open wound in the arm had to do with the hurt and pain between Bobbie and her daughter. I knew the ghost with the vials of infections had to do with their son's ear infections. I also knew the chains had to do with Hal and Bobbie's financial situation. I called Hal the next day and asked if I could meet with him and Bobbie and share what God had showed me in prayer for them the night before by the gifts of the word of knowledge and discerning of spirits.

Taking Authority

I met them at their home, shared this with them and encouraged Hal to take authority over these three spirits. He did and Bobbie and I agreed with him. The results were amazing. That night their son slept all night with no pain for the first time in weeks. Two days later Bobbie's daughter called her and they reconciled. Bobbie did not even know where her daughter was previously or how to contact her. One week later the financial commitment that had been promised to them came through and was more than enough to pay their tuition and meet their needs. Praise God! These victories did not come by my great teaching ability but by the gifts of the word of knowledge and discerning of spirits and taking authority over those demonic spirits attacking them.

I was able to recognize, cooperate with, and operate in these gifts because I had been taught about them and seen them demonstrated in the two Spirit-filled churches I had been a member of just a few years prior to this event. I was not ignorant of these gifts and how they operated. Therefore, Hal and Bobbie were able to receive the benefit of the supernatural power of God. How will you, your friends, or loved ones know to access the gifts of the Spirit when they "hit the wall" in their lives if they never see it demonstrated or taught in a public setting?

Paul told the church at Corinth they came behind in no gift, see First Corinthians 1:7. The reality in the spiritual lives of many Christians today is they come behind in most of the gifts. In fact, many Christians don't even know what each of the nine gifts of the

Spirit are, much less how they operate. And much of this is a result of having no reference point for the gifts in either demonstration or teaching in their church.

This is not a condemnation to any pastor or leader, rather a challenge to return to the foundational patterns and principles of the early church and the book of Acts—maintaining a balance of the Word and the Spirit. Kenneth E. Hagin, a true prophet of God and excellent teacher of the Word, spent the last seven to ten years of his life and ministry urging the pastors and graduates of the Bible school he founded to give place to the move of the Spirit and the gifts of the Spirit in their churches and ministries.

He saw the pendulum swinging too far in the wrong direction away from the things of the Spirit. He warned the church there would be an entire generation who would miss the move of God because pastors and leaders were over-correcting to avoid the abuse of the gifts. My observation is many Christians and churches are in that condition Brother Hagin saw and warned of—ignorant of the gifts and supernatural power of God available to them. They have a form of godliness but deny the power thereof. I have good news for you! It's not too late. God is still moving and we can turn the tide of ignorance about the gifts of the Spirit and move the pendulum back into balance where it belongs.

As you discover the truth and principles highlighted in each chapter of this book, you will be equipped and empowered to flow in the supernatural. Natural limitations of your gifts and resources will be removed. The truths I share come from more than forty years of ministry experience operating in the gifts and receiving revelation from the Word that have been proven. My prayer for you is you will learn to flow in the supernatural and operate the gifts in confidence and biblical order. I believe together we can restore a genuine move of God in the church and world today!

Chapter 3

You Still Have Flesh to Deal With

In the first Spirit-filled church my wife and I attended, we observed a number of various types of demonstrations. But we had no reference point other than what we had read in the Word which of these were of the Spirit and which were just people's flesh. Having been raised in a single-parent home without the regular input from my dad, I had developed a passion to live my life in wisdom and truth. This had been a void in my life and created a strong desire in me to be clear about which demonstrations where legitimate and valid and which were not.

In this church, we observed "Jericho marches" where people marched around seven times over properties they were claiming, people who were sick, and many other situations where they desired breakthroughs. We also observed people who would respond to the Spirit with spiritual "twitching" or contortions each time they sensed Him move upon them. I am not condemning or judging any of these actions or individuals. But this did cause me to seek the Lord, receive counsel from my pastor and spiritual leaders, and search out the Word to discover how to discern which demonstrations were valid and which were not.

What we did find out during this time of seeking the Lord is not everything that moved was moved by the Spirit and not every message with a "thus saith the Lord" on the end of it was actually the Lord speaking. Paul addresses this in his second statement intended to keep us from remaining ignorant about the things of the Spirit:

> *You know that you were Gentiles, carried away to these dumb idols, however you were led* (1 Corinthians 12:2).

What is Paul saying here and what does this have to do with operating in the gifts of the Spirit? He is reminding them and us that even though we are born again and filled with the Spirit, each of us still has the capacity to be led by the flesh. His reference to being led and carried away by dumb idols has to do with the dumb idols or sin patterns of your old life that your flesh still has an inclination to follow. This is true even though your old nature and old man is dead. It is our choice to be led by either the Spirit or the flesh.

When operating the gifts, each of us must realize even the most mature person can be led by his or her flesh or emotions. People may actually be hearing God but process what they hear through the lens of their emotions or flesh. Everything spoken or demonstrated as one of the gifts of the Spirit by believers with a "thus saith the Lord" on the end of it does not automatically make it a "word" from God. It must be judged by the written Word, by mature members and leaders in the church, and confirmed in your heart before acting on it.

Abuse of the Gifts

Most abuse of the gifts that cause pastors and church leaders to shut down the operation of the gifts in their services are the result of well-intentioned people yielding to their flesh or emotions and calling it the Spirit. Every church or ministry that provides opportunity for people to operate in the gifts has experienced this. After I graduated from Bible college, I served as the senior pastor of two Spirit-filled churches in Texas for a total of twenty-seven years. In that period of time I observed many good, powerful, and genuine manifestations of the Spirit. I also observed a number of people attempting to move in the Spirit with some manifestation that was obviously the flesh—obvious to everyone except the person manifesting it.

It is highly probable you have observed some of these manifestations if you have been around the Charismatic "zoo" of gift abuses in church before. First, there is the tambourine lady who comes to every Spirit-filled church and plays her tambourine without permission—in the name of the Lord, of course. And she is always a half a beat off from the worship team. You may have also experienced the "shofar" brothers who blow their shofars at will, unannounced, and frighten those around them. Then there are the flag and banner people who pull out their flags and banners without notice and inadvertently run into or hit their fellow worshipers with their flags or banners.

You may also have seen the dancers who always feel led to go to the front of the auditorium and twirl and swirl to their heart's desire. Or you may have observed someone giving out a harsh and

29

angry sounding tongue or prophetic word. Then there are the "quakers and shakers" who always must shake and quake uncontrollably while giving out a message in tongues or prophecy to attempt to convince all present the Spirit has come upon them. Then there is Mr. or Mrs. Self-appointed Prophet of the house who feels compelled to give out a prophecy in every service and sometimes two or three prophecies per service. And they always have a word for someone every time they come to church.

These are examples of a number of fairly common manifestations that have been subject to abuse by believers with good hearts and intentions but led by the flesh nonetheless. Am I saying that every time someone functions in one of the above manifestations it is their flesh leading them? Absolutely not! Most of the examples I used can be manifestations that are truly led by the Spirit and a real blessing to the church and unbelievers who observe them.

Instead of becoming offended by me bringing these examples out, I encourage you to learn and grow so the true manifestations of the Spirit will draw people to Jesus and not yourself. Paul is telling us in order to have a true move of the Spirit and real manifestations of the gifts, we must acknowledge each of us has to deal with our flesh. We must circumcise our hearts from the tendencies of our flesh to use the gifts to either promote our own personal agenda or meet a need of approval, recognition, or attention from others.

If you are pushy, impatient, and easily offended when attempting to operate in the gifts, your flesh is still leading and dominating you. You are not the only one who has something significant to share. And your greatest safeguard from allowing your flesh to lead you and deceive you in your demonstration of the gifts is being submitted to your pastor, elders, or ministry leaders. Let's look at Paul's instruction regarding order in the release of the gifts in chapter 14 of First Corinthians:

Let two or three prophets speak, and let the others judge. But if anything is revealed to another who sits by, let the first keep silent. For you can all prophesy one by one, that all may learn and all may be encouraged. Or did the word of God come originally from you? Or was it you only that it reached? If anyone thinks himself to be a prophet or spiritual, let him acknowledge that the things which I write to you are the commandments of the Lord. But if anyone is ignorant, let him be ignorant (1 Corinthians 14:29-31, 36-38).

These verses clearly reveal that no individual has the last word when it comes to operating in the gifts of the Spirit. Each person who feels led to step out and operate in the gifts must submit whatever they have to share or manifest to other mature believers and spiritual leaders. In other words, you cannot use the "God card" as an excuse to do and say whatever you want and fail to submit to others, especially delegated spiritual leaders. That is out of order and a fleshly demonstration of the gifts. It also keeps you ignorant of the genuine, spiritual demonstration of the gifts, as is described in verse 38. And Paul tells us in verse 1 that God does not want us to remain ignorant of how these gifts are intended to operate.

Ginny

Years ago in one of the churches I pastored in Texas, a very mature and godly couple began attending our church. They had been involved in ministry and faithful members of a church in another city. They had moved to our area and became involved in our church. The wife, Ginny, was very prophetic and given to prayer and personal ministry to others. Her husband, Ted, was a wonderful servant and became involved in our men's and helps ministry.

After they had joined the church and been members for about a year, I noticed that Ginny was attempting to minister to and connect with various first-time guests to our church at the end of each service. At first I didn't think much of it, being glad one of our members was reaching out to minister to others. However, after a period of time I had a number of my leaders come to me individually sharing the same concern about the way Ginny was ministering to these guests. They had also observed that most of these guests she ministered to did not return to our church.

I decided to ask my wife to help me observe how she ministered to people at the end of the next service. What we saw caused us much concern. She walked up to a new couple and asked if she could pray for them. When they agreed, she grabbed both of their hands, closed her eyes, looked down, and began to pray out loud in tongues. She kept this up for at least five minutes moving back and forth with her head and body and jerking their hands back and forth. After five or six minutes she finally said a few words of interpretation in English that were good words but by this time this man and his wife were looking for the exit door!

I did not do anything immediately about this. I took some time to pray over this and to receive counsel from the elders in my church. They all agreed this came from a good intention of Ginny's heart to minister to others. But they also agreed this was out of order and was not producing the fruit she or we as a church intended. One of the elders related to me she had also been doing this with some of our guest ministers and he did not feel it represented us very well. I am typically very careful and patient when it comes to bringing correction in this area because I want to encourage the operation of the gifts and not quench the Spirit. But in this case there was a strong consensus we needed to confront Ginny about this.

I called Ted on the phone and let him know Janice and I needed to meet with him and Ginny, or just Ginny, about the way she was releasing her ministry to the new people in the church. He gave us permission to meet with her because he had been observing the same things as a bystander. He agreed something needed to be done about this. He also told me he didn't know how to bring correction to her about it without her accusing him of quenching the Spirit in her.

When we met with Ginny, I began by letting her know we appreciated her heart to minister to others and to operate in the gifts of the Spirit. I went on to let her know we believed her intentions were right but her methods of moving in the Spirit were not effective and were creating the wrong fruit and results in the people she was ministering to. She began to weep uncontrollably for several minutes and then told me, "Pastor, you are grievinggggg the Holy Spirittttt!" She intentionally dragged out both words to make sure I understood my mistake in bringing correction to her.

I responded immediately to her, "No Ginny, you are!" I calmly, gently, yet firmly told her the elders and I were responsible to establish proper biblical order for the release of the gifts in our church as we understood it from God's Word. I also told her I understood if she did not agree with the guidelines we had established but that did not change our decision. I let her know we wanted to see people ministered to, but she would not be allowed to minister to new people in our church for a period of time. Then later she would need to take one of the elders or elder's wives with her so what she shared could be judged according to the Word. I also asked her if she did pray in tongues, make it very short and get to the word God had given her for the people she was ministering to as soon as possible. I also asked her to stop all the "gyrations" back and forth when she ministered to others.

Ginny wept some more after we spoke with her, but to her credit she agreed to follow our instructions. She became a much more effective minister to others as a result. Ted was thrilled because he did not know how to lead his wife in this area. This confrontation gave him some direction in his spiritual leadership in their marriage.

This is one painful, but practical example of how people who want to operate in the gifts can yield to their flesh and think it is the Lord. Ginny meant well but *her prophetic gifting needed to be pastored.* It was painful for Ginny because she had to realize her methods were hurting rather than helping people as she intended. It was also painful for her because she had to choose to receive correction without receiving it as personal rejection.

It was certainly painful and confusing to the guest families who had been recipients of Ginny's ministry methods and no doubt caused some to question the legitimacy of the gifts of the Spirit. It was painful for Janice and I and our elders because our willingness to bring correction meant we would run the risk of Ginny and Ted leaving the church. This is one of the reasons pastors and leaders choose to "clamp down" or restrict the gifts of the Spirit in the body, especially in the corporate gathering. In order to have a church where the gifts are demonstrated, the pastor and leaders must be willing to lead and confront people who are operating the gifts in an unprofitable way and risk losing them.

Biblical Confrontation

In short, in order to have a genuine move of God in your church or small group, you have to be willing to lose people. The goal is not losing people but leading people, saving people, and redeeming challenging situations. You have to count biblical confrontation and the potential of losing the individual or family you confront as part of the cost to establish an environment where the gifts operate in biblical order. This is true in a large corporate church setting and in a small group setting, like a home Bible study. Every group will have to deal with strong, dominating personalities and prophetically gifted people who live to share the latest word they hear from God.

Most of the time it is not necessary to address or confront a dominating individual in your group or church publicly. I have trained my leaders to wait until this dominator tries to take charge or interrupt two or three times before getting with them personally. I instruct them to put guidelines on this individual such as: "The next time we meet together in our small group you have only two opportunities to make comments and keep your comments to two minutes in length." Or if in a Sunday morning church service, "For the next month I am asking you not to give out a prophecy or tongue in the service. Then after that you have two opportunities per month, so make them good."

Either I or one of my leaders will appeal to them to trust our leadership and help us establish an environment where many can operate in the gifts and not just a few. Early on in my ministry a man in my church took it upon himself to speak a prophecy every time there was any lull in the service. He was a very gifted communicator and most of the time shared encouraging and timely words from the Lord. The problem was he would speak two or three prophecies per service. Because he was more developed in this gift than others in our church, no one else would ever yield to the Spirit's promptings and step out in the gifts. What's more, this individual would not give anyone else any time to respond to the Lord. He was always ready to prophesy like a race horse out of the gate.

After several weeks of this, and after taking time to pray and receive counsel, I went to him and asked him to help me steward the move of God and the release of the gifts through others in our church. I asked him not to prophesy in our services for the next month and then only twice per month after that. He was a very mature leader and prophet in development and followed my instruction. As a result, we experienced an increase in the operation of the gifts through others in our church.

His Presence a Priority

I love prophetically gifted people. I love their passion to hear God, to pray and worship and spend time in His presence. They challenge me to keep the main thing the main thing: keeping Jesus my first love and making His presence a priority in my life. But prophetically motivated people and prophets need to be pastored. Their downside is they tend to be pushy, like an "eighteen-wheeler" truck on your tail driving down the highway. There is never enough move of God, gifts manifested, or worship to their liking.

They also tend to bring a book of "words" the Lord has been speaking to them they expect me to review. I tell them to condense it to one page before bringing it to me to review because I don't have time to read their book of "words." We must lead prophetic people because they have flesh as well and they can become immersed in their view of what God wants to do in the church and attempt to move the church in that direction through their use of the gifts.

The bottom line, there is a price to pay to have a move of the Spirit and the gifts of the Spirit operate in an orderly way in any church, small group, or ministry. We have to realize it is possible for even mature believers to hear something from the Lord but interpret it through the lens of their emotions or flesh and try to push that through in a way that is not Christlike. This requires each of us to maintain a submissive heart toward spiritual leadership and to realize none of us has all the truth or the last word on any subject. This is true even though we have heard the Lord and are attempting to follow His initiative in operating in the gifts.

For we know in part and we prophesy in part (1 Corinthians 13:9).

In the next chapter we will cover in detail the determining factor of whether a gift or manifestation is being operated in the Spirit or motivated and initiated by the flesh. In any case, having a church or ministry where the gifts are in operation can be messy. It is actually easier on the pastor or spiritual leaders of a church or ministry to shut down the use of the gifts and the move of the Spirit than to have to deal with some of the challenges that arise because of people operating the gifts in the flesh. But I don't see that being the case in the book of Acts or in any of the New Testament epistles to the local churches.

I agree with a statement Kenneth Hagin made many times while teaching on this subject, "I would rather have a little wild fire than the order of a funeral dirge and no fire at all." I believe it is possible to have a move of the Spirit in our lives that blesses others, ministers freedom to the captives, and doesn't leave people, the church, or church leaders in a mess.

Chapter 4

JESUS IS THE CENTER OF ALL THE SPIRIT SAYS AND DOES

IN THE FIRST THREE CHURCHES I ATTENDED AS A YOUNG PERSON, there were almost zero manifestations or demonstrations of the Spirit. But that was not the case in the first Spirit-filled church we joined. There were demonstrations and manifestations that abounded in every service. I shared with you in the last chapter the great passion I had to know which of these demonstrations and manifestations were of the Lord and which were just people's flesh. The principle Paul addresses next and is highlighted in this chapter has been a major revelation that has helped me greatly over the years in making this distinction.

Therefore I make known to you that no one speaking by the Spirit of God calls Jesus accursed, and no one can say that Jesus is Lord except by the Holy Spirit (1 Corinthians 12:3).

There are several things we could take time to unpack from this verse. But the key principle or takeaway is *Jesus is the center of all the Spirit says and does.* In other words, all of the gifts and manifestations of the Spirit will ultimately magnify Jesus and draw attention to Jesus, not ourselves. If a manifestation or demonstration centers on and draws attention more to you and me than Jesus, it is a manifestation of our flesh, not the Spirit. This is the primary determining factor of whether a gift is of the Spirit or of the flesh.

For the testimony of Jesus is the spirit of prophecy (Revelation 19:10).

The Spirit, through His various manifestations will always reveal some facet of Jesus—His love, nature, character, and power. True gifts of the Spirit in operation through you and me will testify of and point people to Jesus, not us. They reveal Jesus' mind, purpose, and heart of love toward people. The gifts are actually all different manifestations of His love for people and His desire for them to walk in freedom and intimate relationship with Him.

However, when He, the Spirit of Truth, has come...He will glorify Me, for He will take of what is Mine and declare it to you (John 16:13-14).

Jesus is telling us here that the Prompter and Initiator of all the gifts, the Holy Spirit, will not prompt us to say or do anything that doesn't glorify and magnify Him. These Scriptures I shared with you make it very clear how we are to determine whether a gift is manifesting from the initiative of the Spirit or from someone's flesh. Is this manifestation or demonstration drawing attention to Jesus or the individual manifesting it? That is such a simple but very powerful truth!

It is also helpful for us in learning to cooperate with the Holy Spirit and submit to spiritual leaders in operating the gifts in biblical order. This is a much better option than remaining zealous to operate in the gifts but ignorant and becoming part of the abuse and mess pastors have to deal with when the gifts are allowed to function out of order. Understanding this principle helped me tremendously as a pastor to establish an environment where the gifts functioned in biblical order while not quenching the Spirit.

I am going to share a few examples of manifestations that occurred in our church over the years we determined were out of order. Understanding this principle that Jesus is the center of all the Spirit says and does was key to helping my leadership team and I know what to address regarding these manifestations in our church.

Out of Order

One Sunday morning during our worship time, one of the ladies in our church went to the front of the auditorium and began to dance and twirl across the front of the stage. I noticed she had a different type of dress on than she normally wore—one that was more formal and one that allowed her more freedom to twirl and swirl around while she danced. She danced throughout one worship song. I didn't think much of it until the next Sunday morning she got up again at the same time during worship and had on the same dress. This time she danced, twirling and swirling, during two worship songs. And of course, she did this in front of the church down by the platform.

I still didn't think or say much about this demonstration of dance she had done the past two weeks. The first time it seemed to bless the people, but the second time it seemed a bit weird and strange to me. It didn't seem to fit in the service, bless the people, or bring glory to the Lord to the same degree it had the week before. The following Sunday she came down to the front again in the same flowing dress, dancing and twirling and swirling to her heart's desire through two worship songs and half of another. By this Sunday morning service all eyes in the church were on the dancer, not the Lord, and I knew I would have to address her in private.

Again, I took some time to pray and seek the Lord about this and also received counsel from my staff and elders. I wanted to make sure it was impacting others the same as it had me. Each church leader I spoke with about this, as well as my wife, agreed we needed to address this lady regarding her choice to dance at the front of the auditorium during worship every service. We decided to ask her to dance in the back of the auditorium any time she felt the Lord was leading her to dance rather than the front so as not to distract people in their worship.

I asked an elder and his wife who had relationship with her to speak with her about this. She did not take it well. She wept and wept and told my elder and his wife we were grieving the Spirit by asking her to do this in the back of the church auditorium. She used the Bible example of David dancing before the Lord and said the Lord led her to do this. She said she was worshiping the Lord through her dance and was influencing many more people in our church to worship than had engaged in worship prior to her dancing up front. Essentially, she had taken it upon herself to become the new worship leader to promote worship in our church through her dance. And she justified this because from her perspective the percentage of individuals engaging in worship was not where she thought it should be.

She and her husband eventually left the church offended over our request to operate her gift in the way we believed was best for our church. Let me make it clear: I am not against dancing before the Lord either privately or in public as a form of worship. I have done that personally in both settings. My heart and the heart of the leaders in our church for individuals engaging in worship is a priority to us. One of the words for worship in the Greek language is *proskuneo*. It means to advance toward as if to kiss. Ephesians 5:22-32 provides a strong analogy between the marriage relationship and our relationship with the Lord.

In my marriage relationship with my wife, whenever I advance toward her to kiss her, I am not thinking about you or anyone else. My focus is on her. In a similar way, our worship time with the Lord should be unbroken intimacy with Him where He is our primary focus. As spiritual leaders, it is our responsibility to make sure our corporate worship times facilitate unbroken intimacy with the Lord for the people. Anything that disturbs that intimacy or draws people's attention off the Lord needs to be addressed.

That is what we did with this precious lady. We did not question her heart of worshiping the Lord through her dance. But it became evident to all except her that her well-intentioned efforts to draw people into worship were actually drawing people's attention off the Lord and toward her dancing. It became a show instead of worship. Remember I said anytime a pastor or spiritual leader addresses someone about operating the gifts in a way they determine is not centered on Jesus, they have to be willing to lose that person out of their congregation. It is not that they are trying to run people off. But these types of confrontations are necessary to establish an environment where the gifts operate in order.

Newfound Freedom

A number of months after this event there was a new couple who began attending our services who had recently come out of a denominational church that did not believe in the gifts of the Spirit. They were both recently filled with the Spirit and were ecstatic about their discovery of the gifts available to them. They were also thrilled about their newfound freedom to operate in the gifts as we gave liberty for people to do so. The husband, I will call Monty, was especially bold to step out in giving messages in tongues.

Monty started giving out messages in tongues in the small group they were attending. His small group leader did not tell me initially about the problem we discovered later in the way he delivered these messages in tongues. The first time I heard him do this was in a Sunday evening service that was designated a worship night. In these services we would spend time in the presence of God, worship, and allow the gifts to flow through the people. When Monty delivered his message in tongues it was very loud and given in a harsh and angry tone. Then he seemed overcome with emotion and exhaustion like he had just finished a 5k race.

After observing this I spoke with his small group leader and asked if Monty had been giving out messages in tongues in his group. He told me he had done that every meeting since he began attending. I asked him if there was anything unique or different about the way he gave these messages in tongues from his perspective. He described the same things I had observed—loud, angry tone, and overcome with emotion. I asked him what impact or effect this seemed to have on the people and the meetings. He said it seemed to bring a heaviness over the people and it would take a while to turn things around spiritually.

I decided to wait and pray over this before saying anything to Monty. The next Sunday morning he gave a message in tongues again and it was the same thing—very loud, harsh and angry tone, and when he finished he seemed exhausted and overcome with emotion. I watched the response of the people after the message was given. Though the interpretation was good, there wasn't the uplifting or encouraging spirit that tongues and interpretation in tongues or prophecy usually has on the people and the service. The overall impact of Monty's use of tongues was it did not manifest or represent Jesus well and it was not benefiting the people.

We established gatekeepers in our church services who were mature men and women of God, usually elders and recognized and proven leaders. The congregation knew if anyone had a word, a message in tongues, or something they felt led to share with the body they should go to one of the gatekeepers and run it by them first before sharing what they sensed they had from the Lord. I asked one of the gatekeepers and Monty's small group leader to meet with Monty and help him grow in his use of the gifts. Monty's first response to them was he could not control himself. He said he had to do it the way the Spirit was moving on him. They shared the following Scripture verse with him:

> *And the spirits of the prophets are subject to the prophets*
> (1 Corinthians 14:32).

It is clear from this verse we can control ourselves. The Holy Spirit does not move on us in such a way where He either forces us to speak or pushes us to do things beyond our control. These two leaders were able to let Monty know though his heart was right, he was not manifesting Jesus by his delivery of the gifts in an angry, harsh tone. They also let him know the impact this was having on the people was not positive. They spent time meeting with him and discipling him. Thankfully Monty began to grow in his understanding of the operation of the gifts and his ministry to others. He learned Jesus is the center of all the Spirit says and does in the church. And his operation in the gifts later became a great blessing to others.

Love Trumps Liberty

One final example of this principle I will share with you happened just a few years before I turned my church over to a son in the faith. I was on vacation one Sunday morning and I received an urgent text from my executive pastor. He said some of our prayer team had come out in the middle of the worship service waving flags and banners across the front of the stage and he didn't know what to do. This was a surprise to me as well because none of these prayer team members had notified me or our staff of their intentions to worship with banners and flags.

I told my executive pastor not to do anything about the flags and banners right then. I let him know once the worship time was complete they would sit down and we could deal with this at a later time.

I want to share an important principle with pastors and leaders right now. One service where things don't go as planned or something is manifest out of order will not destroy your church! In most cases it is not necessary to correct these things publicly. It is only what you tolerate on a consistent basis that will impact your church in a negative way.

When I returned from my vacation, I spoke with my executive pastor about what happened the previous week, but we did not have time to address it before the next service. The leader of our prayer ministry, a woman I will call Trudy, was the one responsible for providing the flags and banners to others. The next Sunday morning was Easter Sunday. At the beginning of the worship time, Trudy and her team came out of the prayer room with flags and banners waving them around back and forth in both the front and back of the church. This week they had several children they gave banners and ribbons to in addition to the flags. Two major problems occurred as I observed all the banners and flags waving.

First, several of the children and one or two of the adults were running into people entering the church service and people were having to duck their heads to avoid being hit by the flags, banners, or flagpoles. Second, the majority of the people, including the worship team, were riveted on all the flags and banners waving. I later met with my elders and after prayer we all agreed flags and banners in our church setting did not facilitate worship among our people.

I called Trudy and her husband into my office the next week and told her I appreciated her passion to worship the Lord and knew she and most of those whom she had given flags and banners to were worshiping the Lord. But I let her know we had decided because of the size of our auditorium and the effect we observed the banners and flags had on our people, this was not something we would be doing on a regular basis. I let her know from our perspective it was not facilitating true worship among our people. Rather it was distracting people from their worship of God even though her intention was something different.

I let Trudy and her husband know of a couple of churches in the area that welcomed flags and banners and encouraged them to check those out if she felt she needed to worship God this way. A few weeks later, with our blessing, they did leave the church for another church with that type of worship vision.

There is an important principle I want to point out here if you desire to flow in the supernatural and move with confidence in operating in the gifts. *An individual's personal liberty to operate in the gifts is not a trumping value over love.* In other words, your right to operate in the gifts is not greater than what is in the best interest of the whole body. Whether you are part of a small group or a large church, it is the pastor or spiritual leader's responsibility to regulate the manifestations of the gifts.

The way they are to do that is to determine if the manifestation points people to Jesus or draws attention to themselves. They also can observe the fruit or effects these manifestations have on the people. It is their responsibility to make sure these gifts manifest Jesus and produce good fruit in the body more than meeting the need of the one manifesting the gift. Sad to say that some minister to others out of a need to be needed. And that it is all about themselves, rather than blessing and encouraging others. I encourage you to make it your goal to bless others with your gifts by making Jesus the center of all you say and do and by submitting to mature, spiritual leaders in your life.

Chapter 5

BE OPEN TO THE UNFAMILIAR NOT THE UNBIBLICAL

As I began to grow in my walk of learning to flow in the supernatural, I discovered a common "sticking point" or hindrance most people deal with when starting to move out in the gifts of the Spirit. That hindrance is being hesitant to receive from certain ministries because the way they operate the gifts is unfamiliar to them.

When I first moved to Decatur, Texas, to assume my second assignment as pastor of a church there, I reached out to a number of pastors in the area. One of the pastors I met and connected with I will call Phil. Phil and I connected immediately and he, one other pastor in the area, and I began to meet together once a week for coffee, prayer, and fellowship.

Phil was really hungry for God and the move of the Spirit. He had come out of a denomination that did not believe in healing, the gifts of the Spirit, or the Baptism in the Holy Spirit. He had recently been filled with the Spirit and was like a child in a candy store where it came to healing, the gifts of the Spirit, and the supernatural power of God. He attended every conference and meeting by every healing evangelist and minister who moved in signs and wonders within one hundred miles of our area.

During one of our weekly pastor's fellowship meetings, Phil came in with some serious questions for us. He had attended a healing meeting with a renowned healing evangelist in the area the weekend before and was very disturbed about what he had observed. He said in one of the services he was in, the evangelist did not even preach the Word. He said all he did was lead the congregation in worship and call out a few specific types of diseases people were being healed of. Then people started coming forward for either prayer or to testify of their healing. He said the thing that upset him most was when people came up on the stage, the evangelist blew on them to receive their healing. The other thing he did not understand is why everyone he blew on fell down or fell out in the Spirit.

He declared to me and the other pastor at our meeting, "Doesn't the Bible say they shall lay hands on the sick and they will recover? He didn't lay hands on anyone. He just blew on them!" Phil was a real "Word man" and he had to see it in the Bible before he would believe it was real. I admired him for that. What we shared with Phil I believe will help you if you desire to operate in the gifts and the supernatural.

First we explained to Phil, though the Bible does say the Lord will confirm His Word with signs following, He is not limited in the way He gets healing to people. God loves people so much He gave us gifts of healings, working of miracles, and the gift of faith. He gave us these gifts, members of His body who can operate in these gifts, as well as healing evangelists to help people who don't have time to hear messages on healing or meditate the on Word and receive that way. Some people who only have a short time to live, are ravaged by disease, and are taking so much pain medication they cannot focus on the Word, need the gifts of the Spirit.

Let me share a brief aside here. For those in these type of situations, I still encourage family and friends to play teaching, faith-filled messages on healing in the room where your suffering loved one is. The person's body and mind may not be functioning at full capacity but their spirit man can still receive the Word!

Now back to this story. We told Phil, "Thank God for the gifts of the Spirit and the healing evangelist even if he doesn't operate his ministry the way we would in that situation." We asked him, "Was anyone healed at this meeting?" He told us indeed there were scores of people healed.

We asked him, "Was anyone saved at this meeting?" He affirmed to us again more people than he could count received the Lord that night. My other pastor friend and I proclaimed together at the same time, "Well, praise God! God healed scores of people and saved multitudes of people and did it different from how you would have. That just proves He doesn't need our permission to do what we all want Him to do in a different way from what we are familiar with." This seemed to help Phil and settle him down. I then shared a passage of Scripture with him that is found in First Corinthians chapter 12:

> *There are diversities of gifts, but the same Spirit. There are differences of ministries, but the same Lord. And*

there are diversities of activities, but it is the same God who works all in all (1 Corinthians 12:4-6).

I told Phil these verses have helped me stay open to different gifts, different ministries, and different operations of the gifts. I told him the way the Lord interpreted these verses to me is, "There are different gifts that different ministries operate in different ways. But it is the same God who is working through each of them." When I shared this with Phil, it was like a light bulb turned on in his heart and he saw it. I went on to tell him these verses were written in the context of instruction to us about the gifts of the Spirit. This is a clear admonition by the Lord for us to *stay open to the unfamiliar, but not unbiblical* demonstrations of the Spirit when learning to function in these gifts.

Stay Open to Gifts

I believe it is also implied if we don't stay open to gifts that are operated different from what we are familiar or comfortable with, we will stay ignorant of the various ways He moves through the gifts. Don't close your heart to new or different manifestations of the Spirit unless they violate the Word. Our other pastor friend who was at this meeting gave Phil the following Scriptures:

> *And when He had said this, He breathed on them, and said to them, "Receive the Holy Spirit"* (John 20:22).

> *And the Lord God formed man of the dust of the ground, and breathed into his nostrils the breath of life; and man became a living being* (Genesis 2:7).

He said, "Look here in the Word. Jesus blew, breathed, on people and God blew, breathed, on people." He told Phil he did not operate the way this evangelist did by blowing on people to receive healing and he also was not advocating this for others. But at least there is scriptural precedence for it. In other words, though it was unfamiliar to Phil, it was not unbiblical.

After sharing these things with Pastor Phil, he was very encouraged and blessed and had new understanding and appreciation for the things of the Spirit. What Pastor Phil learned that day is something each of us needs to understand in order to flow in the supernatural in new dimensions—*different ministries operate different gifts in different ways.* We need to be careful about judging or despising others who operate in the gifts and flow in the supernatural different from ourselves or our group. What people are not up on, they are usually down on and critical of.

We need to guard ourselves from closing our hearts to new or different manifestations of the Spirit unless they violate the Word. Whether it is laughing, falling, dancing, shouting, running, prophesying, or giving out a message in tongues or interpretation of tongues, these are all in the Bible. If it is in the Word of God, or at least doesn't violate the Word, we need to be open to it.

A minister friend of mine, Dave Duell, had a very unique way of ministering healing and deliverance to people. I met Dave at an Andrew Wommack ministers' conference in 1994. Dave told the story of how the Lord spoke to him that his arm and hand would act like a sword in the Spirit realm and cut chains and cords of bondage off people whenever he prayed for them. Dave would make weird noises and chopping motions with his hands and people would fall out in the Spirit, be healed and set free. He was a genuine healing evangelist equipped with gifts of healings who saw multitudes of people saved, healed, delivered, and filled with the Spirit.

The first time an individual experienced Dave's unique ministry, they could be tempted to turn him off because the methods God led him to manifest the gifts were different from most. But if you understand the primary principle of this chapter—different ministries operate different gifts in different ways—you remain open, learn, and receive. My daughter-in-law, Jessica, went forward in one of Dave's meetings in Chico, Texas, where one of my sons in the faith, Donald McMaster, was pastor. She responded to Dave's invitation to be filled with the Spirit.

After she received the wonderful Baptism in the Holy Spirit with the evidence of speaking in other tongues, she started to return to her seat. Dave, by the leading of the Spirit, asked her to stop. He said the Lord had more for her, that He had healing for her. He used his arm to chop all chains of infirmity and sickness off her and she fell to the floor immediately. She could not get up for close to an hour and all she could say was, "My stomach is shaking and quivering and it won't stop."

What Dave did not know was Jessica had been to the doctor just that week and a sonogram revealed scar tissue from cancer surgery and treatments she had several years before. The doctor told her because of this she could not have any more children. After this service that Dave prayed for her, Jessica decided to go back to the doctor because she was certain she was healed. The doctor did another sonogram and was shocked by the results. He asked her, "What has happened to you? You look like you have had an internal makeover. You have no more scar tissue!"

Jessica replied, "I know what has happened to me. Jesus has healed me!" Needless to say our entire family was ecstatic. And we have three more grandchildren now as a result of this healing miracle and Dave's unique ministry gift. The Bible speaks many times of the arm of the Lord representing the power of God (Isaiah 53:1). God used Dave's arm in a unique way to release healing and miracles—God's power—to people. And one of those people was our daughter-in-law, Jessica, and our family quiver has increased and been blessed because of it. Dave has since gone home to be with Jesus. We miss him and the wonderful way he manifested Jesus' love and healing power to multitudes.

I realize not every manifestation or ministry is genuine, like Dave's was. Each of us is responsible to check these things out by the Word of God and by the fruit that is born by that ministry or ministry gift. You have to ask the questions:

- Is this minister teaching, preaching, and valuing the Word of God?

- Is the unique way the minister is manifesting the gifts in line with the Word?

- Are people being saved, healed, delivered, and being discipled through the ministry?

- Does the ministry draw people to Jesus?

Unbiblical Manifestations

Some examples of unbiblical manifestations I have heard being promoted in some Christian circles are people barking, feathers falling, and gold dust appearing in a service. There was a revival several years ago that started off pure and degraded to a point where some of the people began barking like dogs in their services. I cannot judge that movement, but I do not see barking in the book of Acts or any epistle in the New Testament. Furthermore, I fail to see the benefit or fruit of that and would declare this a false manifestation.

There was a ministry that moved in the genuine power of God several years ago that saw many salvations and healings. This minister decided to spice the meetings up a bit by releasing feathers in their meetings as a supposed manifestation of the Spirit. It was found sometime later this was being staged and this ministry that was genuine lost its influence. Recently there have been reports of several meetings in churches and ministries where gold dust has appeared. Some close associates of mine have asked me about this. I cannot see this manifestation in the New Testament and neither can I see the benefit of this unless the participants in the meetings could somehow package the gold dust and sell it.

Just because we see false manifestations from time to time I encourage you not to throw the baby out with the bathwater. These are counterfeits. A counterfeit reveals there is the true and the genuine. There are real manifestations of the Spirit that the church and the world need today. Jesus preached and taught the Word but He also operated in the gifts of the Spirit and various manifestations of the Spirit. And not every manifestation or demonstration of the Spirit He used was familiar to the people.

Real but Strange Manifestations

Did you know that Jesus had a "spitting ministry?" That's right. Jesus spit on some people to release healing to them. Let's look at this strange manifestation in the Word:

> *And He took him aside from the multitude, and put His fingers in his ears, and He spat and touched his tongue. Then, looking up to heaven, He sighed, and said to him, "Ephphatha," that is, "Be opened." Immediately his ears were opened, and the impediment of his tongue was loosed, and he spoke plainly* (Mark 7:33-35).

> *So He took the blind man by the hand and led him out of the town. And when he had spit on his eyes and put His hands on him, He asked him if he saw anything. …Then He put His hands on his eyes again and made him look*

up. And he was restored and saw everyone clearly (Mark 8:23,25).

In these two accounts Jesus actually spit directly on the recipient of healing. In the first case He spat in His hands and touched the man's tongue with the spit. In the second instance it says Jesus spit on the person's eyes. There is another instance that records He spit on the clay and made mud and put it on the man's eyes but in these two cases there was no dirt or mud involved. In the Old Testament spitting on someone or something was a sign of disdain for them. It could be Jesus' spitting was representative of His disdain for deafness and blindness. But in any case, He, nonetheless, released the healing power of God in this unusual way with these two men.

I am not advocating we pick up Jesus' spitting anointing or gifting. I am pointing this out to show you Jesus did break the mold on normal ministry. He manifested God's healing power in unique, yet genuine and powerful ways. It was even said of His ministry:

We have seen strange things today! (Luke 5:26)

Let's remember as we begin to move in the supernatural and operate His wonderful gifts, He is not limited to our flavor of manifestation or the kind of ministry we are familiar with. Baskin Robbins advertises thirty-one flavors of ice cream. God has more than thirty-one types of ministry and gift demonstrations He can flow through. Different ministries operate different gifts in different ways. Stay open to the unfamiliar but genuine manifestations of the Spirit and your ministry capacity will expand and grow and you will bless many!

Chapter 6

THE GIFTS ARE FOR EVERYONE IN THE BODY

THE NEXT PRINCIPLE OF LEARNING HOW TO FLOW IN THE SUPER-natural and operate in the gifts of the Spirit takes a personal turn. This turn requires each of you to accept responsibility to learn about the gifts and make yourself available to use them in your life and ministry. Let's look at Paul's admonishment to us in this area:

> *But the manifestation of the Spirit is given to each one for the profit of all* (1 Corinthians 12:7).

Notice in this verse Paul says each one of us has been given the manifestation of the Spirit. No one in the body is left out. Operating in the gifts is not just for the "super-dupers" or specially gifted people or ministers. Everyone in the body is supposed to be involved in manifesting the gifts. No one is left out! And he goes on to say when each one is involved in manifesting the gifts all will profit.

As I shared with you earlier in this book, my wife and I were filled with the Spirit in 1976 after listening to a Christian television ministry called the *700 Club*. Soon after we became involved with a Spirit-filled church that taught, modeled, and allowed the gifts of the Spirit to operate. We observed the pastor, leaders, and members of our new church family function in the gifts. We also heard many stories from our pastor, Sunday school teacher, and guest speakers about using the gifts of the Spirit to minister healing and deliverance to many people. This created a hunger and desire in us to be used in the gifts of the Spirit to help hurting people.

One day in October 1976 a friend of mine, I will call Tom, who had been attending our new church at our invitation, called me and sounded very distraught. He said he had been dating a young woman named Deborah and had been sharing the Lord with her. He didn't think she was saved and said every time he began to talk to her about spiritual things, especially when he mentioned Jesus to her, she would start shaking uncontrollably, make shrieks and noises, and act like she was losing her mind. He asked me if he could bring her over to our house to minister to her.

I told Tom with a confident voice, "Sure, bring Deborah over tonight and the Lord will set her free." I was confident on the outside but on the inside I was filled with doubt and fear. We had just been filled with the Spirit for six months. I had heard all the testimonies of others in our church who had ministered freedom to people by the Word and through the gifts of the Spirit. But they all knew the Word better than we did. They all had been filled with the Spirit longer than we had been. And they all had much more experience than we had. I was sorely tempted to call our pastor or one of the church leaders to come over that night and minister freedom to Deborah. I had confidence in their ability to help her but needed to develop confidence in the Lord's ability through me.

Tom brought Deborah over to our house that night and we began by just listening to each of their stories and backgrounds over some coffee and cake. After about thirty minutes of listening, Janice and I began to share about Jesus and the difference He had made in our lives. About five minutes into our sharing of Jesus, Deborah's eyes began to go "wild," moving from side to side. She then started to speak in a different voice than she had been speaking just a few minutes earlier. The voice repeated several times, "Get me out of here. I have to leave this place right now."

Tom, Janice, and I began to pray quietly in the Spirit in between efforts to attempt to calm Deborah down with kind, gentle affirmations of God's love for her. Suddenly she began to roll around on the floor under our living room coffee table making groans and screeching cries. This was something Janice and I had never experienced before, and it caused us to cry out to Jesus to help us help this girl who was being tormented by the devil. We were praying and using the name of Jesus, but she was still writhing around the floor in agony.

After about five minutes of this, which seemed like an eternity, I heard the Spirit speak up in my spirit, "Command the spirit in Deborah to be still and then ask if she wants to be free." I remembered reading in the gospels how Jesus had commanded the spirit in someone to be still so I thought I had nothing to lose by doing what Jesus did. I then spoke up with a loud voice, "I command you evil, confusing spirit in Deborah to be still in Jesus' name." At that very moment Deborah went limp on the floor and stopped rolling around and stopped screaming in agony. I then got down on my knees on the floor and looked into Deborah's eyes and asked her, "Deborah, do you want to be free?"

She said with great emotion, "Yes, please help me." Each of us then commanded that evil spirit in Deborah to come out of her and leave her in Jesus' name. That voice came back through her voice and said, "No, I'm not going and you can't make me leave."

I spoke again to that spirit, "Be still and come out of her now in Jesus' name." Deborah went limp again and then sat up asking us what had happened and how she had ended up on the floor. We explained to her what had happened and asked her if she wanted to receive Jesus and keep the devil out of her life for good. She received the Lord and was filled with the Spirit that night. Praise God! She then became a member of our church, joined the singles' ministry and had a deep passion and hunger to understand the Word.

Deborah became a true disciple of Jesus from a place of real demonic bondage. This would not have happened that night and certainly not through us had we not accepted our responsibility to use the gifts to minister to her. The gift of discerning of spirits manifested that night to show me I was dealing with an evil spirit. And the word of wisdom was in operation to show me what to do to set her free. In subsequent chapters I will explain each of these gifts in greater detail.

Access to the Gifts

Each of the nine wonderful gifts of the Spirit are available to you and to each member of the body of Christ! No one is left out. And these gifts are not optional. They are given to us to use to help people identify the real issues, bondages, and strongholds in their lives and to set them free. Not every individual who needs help will be in the place where Deborah was, but that's my point. Janice and I were novices in the things of the Spirit when we ministered to Deborah. But because we had been taught what the Word says about the gifts and we were members of a church that modeled these things, we were able to access the gifts needed to set this desperate soul free! If we could do that as novices, what can you do to help others who need freedom by simply making yourself available to draw on these nine powerful gifts?

The title of the next chapter in this book is, "How Do I Get Started?" where I describe some practical steps about operating in the gifts on a daily basis. The first step in this process begins in this chapter—believing the gifts are available for you. You will not operate in the gifts with any consistency until you believe they have been given to you to use in your life and ministry. In the remainder of this chapter I share with you some additional scriptural foundation for these gifts being available to each of us. Then I address a couple of passages of Scripture that seem to say the gifts aren't for all of us and have passed away.

> *But one and the same Spirit works all these things, distributing to each one individually as He wills* (1 Corinthians 12:11).

This verse is very clear in describing that the Spirit directs the gifts He wills and knows is best in a particular situation. It also is clear that He distributes these gifts to each of us—*"each one."* Again, no one is left out. We can all operate in the gifts!

> *I wish you all spoke with tongues, but even more that you prophesied...* (1 Corinthians 14:5).

God's desire expressed through Paul here is that all of us spoke with tongues and all of us moved in prophecy.

> *How is it then, brethren? Whenever you come together, each of you has a psalm, has a teaching, has a tongue, has a revelation, has an interpretation. Let all things be done for edification* (1 Corinthians 14:26).

In this verse it is confirmed that every time the church comes together, each member of the body has something to contribute that the Spirit has downloaded and distributed to each one.

For you can all prophesy one by one, that all may learn and all may be encouraged (1 Corinthians 14:31).

Again in this verse it confirms that all can prophesy. The gifts are not just available to a few gifted and special people. All means all and all includes you! Now before we move on to share with you how you can get started developing consistency in the gifts on a regular basis, let me share a couple of passages some have used to teach the gifts are not for all.

Now you are the body of Christ, and members individually. And God has appointed these in the church: first apostles, second prophets, third teachers, after that miracles, then gifts of healings, helps, administrations, varieties of tongues. Are all apostles? Are all prophets? Are all teachers? Are all workers of miracles? Do all have gifts of healings? Do all speak with tongues? Do all interpret? But earnestly desire the best gifts. And yet I show you a more excellent way (1 Corinthians 12:27-31).

This passage of Scripture that is included in Paul's teaching on not being ignorant about the gifts of the Spirit has actually been used by some teachers to discourage the use of the gifts. Let's take a closer look at what Paul by the Spirit is teaching us here. In verse 27 he is declaring each of us as vital members of the body of Christ. No one is more or less important or valuable. That is emphasized in verses 14-26. Yet in verse 28 Paul tells us in spite of the fact each member is valuable, not all have the same calling from God. He says some members of the body have been set and appointed by God in various ministry offices to equip and train other members of the body for their particular work of ministry.

Ministry Offices

Not everyone is called into one of these ministry offices, though He does have a purpose for each of us. It is by God's design and choosing. He then describes some of these ministry offices: apostles, prophets, and teachers. He then mentions miracles and gifts of healings. Though these are two of the gifts of the Spirit available to each of us I am convinced by the context of this passage these refer to the ministry office of the evangelist whose ministry assignment requires these gifts to operate to win the lost.

I am also convinced that *"varieties of tongues"* is part of the pastor's ministry office that he or she must function in if they are to model the appropriate use of the gifts and keep things decent and in order in regard to operating the gifts in the local church. Varieties of tongues includes the interpretation of tongues that is required when a public message in tongues is given. A pastor must step into the grace to interpret a message given in tongues in a service if no one else interprets it. This is part of the equipping of the ministry of a pastor.

The questions asked in verses 29-30 are each rhetorical. The obvious answer is no to each question. The reason the answer to each question is "no" is because not all of us are called to be apostles, prophets, teachers, evangelists, or pastors. These questions are referring to ministry offices and the gifts assigned to those offices, not the nine gifts of the Spirit available to each one of us as a believer. There is a difference between being used in the gifts as a believer and being set in a ministry office that operates in these gifts as part of their ministry function in that office. The gifts typically function in these offices at a higher level of anointing, authority, and power.

Ron and Carolyn Smith were very close ministry friends of ours and our church family when I served as pastor in Decatur, Texas. They trained as associate pastors for fourteen years under Mom and Dad Goodwin in Pasadena, Texas. The Goodwins were known to operate in a very unique ministry of tongues and interpretation of tongues and Ron and Carolyn Smith walked in that same ministry anointing. The Smiths pastored for several years and then had a prophetic traveling ministry in the latter part of their lives. They came to our church annually and this unique and powerful gift of tongues and interpretation of tongues would operate through them in our church and bless our people.

Carolyn would stand up as she was prompted by the Lord and begin to give out a message in tongues. She was typically very demonstrative as she would walk around and make corresponding motions with her arms and hands. Then Ron would follow with the interpretation to her message using almost the exact same motions and actions Carolyn had made during her message in tongues. When the interpretation came, it was very powerful and had a positive and profound impact on the congregation.

I have witnessed literally hundreds of messages in tongues and interpretation of tongues given in churches and small groups in over forty years of Spirit-filled ministry. And most of these have brought encouragement and blessing to God's people who were present. Yet none of these had the same level of anointing and kingdom impact that the ministry of Ron and Carolyn Smith had when they demonstrated these same gifts through their ministry office.

That is the point of the questions in this passage in First Corinthians 12:29-30. Each of us can potentially move out in the Spirit by giving out a public message in tongues and interpretation of tongues. But not all of us are called into a ministry office that uses those gifts in the unique way God designed for these gifts to function as part of the equipping for that ministry.

Another example of this is with the ministry of Dave Duell I shared about earlier in this book. Dave had a unique gift of healing that involved using a chopping motion with his arm to release healing to people. Though each of us can access the gifts of healings to minister healing to people, not all of us can operate in the ministry office and the unique gift of healing the Lord assigned specifically to Dave's ministry office.

Paul amplifies this distinction in verse 31, *"But earnestly desire the best gifts...."* In context, he was saying we can't covet these ministry offices that use the gifts in the unique ways assigned to their ministry, but we can still covet the *best gifts*. The best gifts are the ones needed most at the time to minister God's life, love, and freedom to people. One final thing to note here is Paul didn't ask the question, "Do all function in helps or administrations?" Therefore, these are areas we all will have opportunity to function in and use the gifts in, especially in the ministry of helps.

The other passage some teachers have used to say the gifts are passed away and therefore unessential today is found in the following verses:

> *Love never fails. But whether there are prophecies, they will fail; whether there are tongues, they will cease; whether there is knowledge, it will vanish away. For we know in part and we prophesy in part. But when that which is perfect has come, then that which is in part will be done away* (1 Corinthians 13:8-10).

Again, this passage is in the context of Paul teaching us how not to be ignorant of the operation of the gifts and things of the Spirit.

Why would it be important to teach us how not to be ignorant of the gifts if they were to pass away soon and not be available to us any longer? What I have heard a few teachers relay as their understanding of this passage of Scripture is that the Bible isthe "that which is perfect" that is to come. They go on to say once the canon of New Testament Scripture was complete, we no longer need the gifts because then we no longer know in part.

Yet Paul provides further explanation of the time we will no longer need the gifts and gives further light on what he meant by that which is perfect to come just two verses later in this passage:

> For now we see in a mirror, dimly, but then face to face. Now I know in part, but then I shall know just as I also am known (1 Corinthians 13:12).

This verse makes it very clear the perfect which is to come that Paul was referring to is Jesus at His return. Before His return we see through a glass darkly—we know in part—and therefore need the gifts of the Spirit. When is it we will see Him face to face? When is it we will know Him as we are known by Him with full knowledge so we won't need the gifts of the Spirit anymore? When He returns for us at His second coming.

> They shall see His face, and His name shall be on their foreheads. There shall be no night there: They need no lamp nor light of the sun, for the Lord God gives them light. And they shall reign forever and ever (Revelation 22:4-5).

Jesus is that which is perfect to come that Paul was speaking about in this passage of Scripture. When we see Him face to face at His coming, we won't need the gifts of the Spirit to compensate for our state of "seeing through a glass darkly" now in this world.

We will then have full knowledge of Him—we will *"know as we are known."* Here is the question I want to ask all who have taught that the Bible or canon of the New Testament was what Paul was referring to as that *"which is perfect to come."*

If the Bible was the perfect to come, why would Paul write chapter 14 of First Corinthians about the proper function, order, and operation of the gifts in the church if they were to pass away as soon as it came to the Corinthian church? That just doesn't make sense. No, my dear reader, the Bible, or canon of New Testament Scripture, is not the perfect to come that Paul was speaking about. It is Jesus, upon His return when we see Him face to face and know as we are known, who is the perfect to come.

Until His return we need these precious gifts. They will compensate for our lack of knowledge because the Spirit is the Spirit of truth and He will lead us and guide us into all truth. He will use these nine powerful gifts to assist us when we are in the dark and need help to minister to others. Praise God each of us has access to these gifts and they are for each member of the church today!

Chapter 7

How Do I Get Started?

"Lord, make us a blessing to others today." This is the prayer I heard Kenneth Hagin say he and his wife prayed as they went about their everyday business. He said God honored that prayer by opening up so many divine appointments and ministry opportunities for them. And it wasn't just in large meetings God answered that prayer. Most days it was simply with individuals and one-on-one encounters that were not initially ministry related. But as they listened to and followed the leading of the Spirit, He showed them things about people, what they were going through or dealing with, and He used that to speak to and minister to them.

This is a practice my wife and I have made part of our lives since hearing Brother Hagin's testimony about this. "Lord, make us a blessing to the group we are meeting with today." Or, "Lord, make us a blessing to the individual we are meeting with today." Praying along these lines helps us become more dependent upon and sensitive to the Holy Spirit. It also makes us more open and available to operate in the gifts of the Spirit that are available to each of us.

One morning several years ago after I had prayed this prayer, "Lord, make me a blessing today," I had an appointment with a lady in our church I was not looking forward to. She had been harsh and verbally abusive to several people in our church over several weeks and my associate pastor and I had called her in to confront her about this. I met with my associate pastor prior to this meeting and shared with him how and what I planned to address with her. As soon as she sat down in our meeting, instead of confronting her, I found myself sharing with her how much we appreciated all the various ways she had been serving in the church.

My associate pastor looked at me in amazement. I didn't say a word to her about the things she had said or done in harsh ways with others in our church. Then all of a sudden she burst into tears and said, "I've been so bad and harsh with others, Pastor Greg. I'm so sorry. I'll go to each person and apologize and you have my commitment I won't do that again. I was so sure you were going to condemn me and kick me out of the church today for my actions. I was sitting outside your office today in fear like I was when I sat outside the principal's office in middle school when I was in trouble as a young girl."

Listen to the Holy Spirit

Listening to the Holy Spirit and depending on Him to help you be a blessing will open you up to say and do things by the Spirit that will accomplish so much more than you could by leaning on your own understanding. You can get in on this as well. Begin by simply asking the Holy Spirit to make you a blessing to others each day.

Then be intentional about listening to Him and following His leading in each situation you are in.

This starts by intentionally connecting with and listening to the individuals, people, or group you are with. What is going on with them and what are their needs, desires, or passions? Second, intentionally connect with the Holy Spirit. What is He doing and what is His heart for the individual, people, or group you are with? The reality is He is present with you and me 24/7. The real question is, "Are you present to Him?" Many times we are just present in our own plans and needs.

A number of years ago, my son, Jeremiah, and daughter-in-law, Jessica, were operating out of one car for their family. Jessica would drop off Jeremiah at work about twenty minutes from home and then later in the day pick him up from work. One day as she was supposed to be heading to Jeremiah's workplace to pick him up, she sensed very strongly from the Lord that she should go home first. Her mind fought with this for a little while as this would make her quite late to pick up her husband from work. But she simply followed what she was sensing the Spirit leading her to do. When she got home, she found her eighty-seven-year-old next door neighbor passed out in her front yard from the heat. Because Jessica was more "present to God" than to her schedule, this lady's life was saved. Praise God!

Many times when I am meeting with an individual or in a meeting with a small or large group, I ask the Lord these three questions:

1. "Lord, what are You doing or what do You want to do in this individual's life or in this group?"

2. "Lord, what are You saying or what do You want to say to this individual or to this group?"

3. Lord, what do You want me to say or do in this situation?"

In order to begin being used in the gifts of the Spirit, we simply need to cease being self-absorbed and worried about what will happen to us if we step out and obey the prompting of the Spirit. Most of the time when we move out and follow the leading of the Spirit it is a very low-risk situation. Many times it comes down to something simple like, "Could I pray for you?" or just following some direction you received in prayer.

My wife came to me one morning after a time she had spent in the Word and prayer and announced to me, "While I was in prayer this morning the Lord told me to take Bonnie some toilet paper, light bulbs, and a roast." Bonnie was the wife of one of the leaders in our church who was also a very successful and wealthy business owner. I have learned and experienced over the years when Janice hears something from the Lord as specific as what she shared with me that morning she is almost always "spot on."

However, this particular morning I allowed my pride to challenge the direction she received. I especially was troubled about her taking toilet paper to this lady. But when I stopped to think about why I was troubled about it the reality was I was concerned about what her husband would think of us if my wife gave them toilet paper. Whenever the Lord gives us some direction or prompting to do something for someone or give them a word He has given us for them and we start to consider how this will make us look or feel, we will almost always miss the opportunity to be a blessing to others.

> **THE REALITY IS WE CANNOT BLESS THOSE WE ARE TRYING TO IMPRESS.**

So I quickly relented and encouraged Janice to do what God had instructed her to do in her time of prayer. Janice took the items to Bonnie at her home later that day. When Bonnie saw what Janice brought her she squealed with delight and said, "How did you know I needed these things? I have been sick with the flu for the last three days and had just run out of toilet paper and light bulbs, and I had nothing to fix my husband and family for dinner tonight."

She was so thankful for Janice's care for her and for her obedience to the Lord. She was also very blessed to know and experience the Lord's care and love for her by speaking to someone to bring her things she needed when she was not feeling well enough to get out and shop for them herself. The thing that blessed her most was Janice purchased the exact brand of toilet paper she always purchased for her family!

Important Lessons Learned

I learned some very important lessons about following the Lord's leading in blessing others that day. First, our pride can stop us from being a blessing if we consider ourselves more than others. Second, God will show us ways to bless others if we are open to Him and not lean to our own understanding. Third, most of the time what He leads us to do or say to bless others is very low risk. What would have been the worst thing that could have happened if Bonnie had not needed the specific items Janice brought her that day? She still would have been blessed and thankful that Janice was thinking of her and praying for her.

I have discovered in more than forty years of ministry there are three primary obstacles that hinder people from stepping out in the gifts of the Spirit:

1. Lack of confidence in hearing God's voice—"Was that the Lord or just me?"

2. Fear—"What if I miss it?"

3. Pride—"What will others think of me if miss it, fail, or make a mistake?"

Remember, you and I have prayed at the beginning of each day, "Lord, make me a blessing to others today." After praying that and making yourself available to be a blessing to others and you sense the Lord leading you to do or say something to encourage and bless someone, is that the Lord or just you? It is the Lord in you. We are co-laborers with Him. What if you miss it by stepping out and following the prompting of the Lord in you? The bigger question is what if you miss it by failing to step out and follow the Lord's leading to bless that person or persons?

Is it really all that important what people think of you? If you really knew how little they did think about you, you would not worry about it. Most people are thinking of themselves. We don't want to err by falling into that category. When you are thinking of others, you are thinking like God!

Whatever I am sensing the Lord leading me to do or say to another I ask myself a simple question, "How will this bless them?" If I sense it will be a blessing to them more than a benefit to me, I go for it. What do I have to lose? My reputation? If I am concerned about my reputation, my concerns are about me, not others.

God is love. When love is leading me, I cannot fail. *"Love never fails,"* (1 Corinthians 13:8). When moving out in the gifts of the Spirit—whether prophecy, a word of knowledge, a word of wisdom, gifts of healings, etc.—you almost always have to act against fear and pride. You do this by focusing on benefiting another rather than the impact on yourself. Fear and pride are borne out of self-ishness, and these are enemies of love.

His Voice

When my youngest son, Jeremiah, was seven years of age, he came home from a friend's house and shared a very interesting event that happened there that day. We had given him permission to go over to his friend David's house, which was just down the street from our house. Jeremiah told me while he was playing with David in their living room, he heard the Lord speak to him, "Go stand behind Ariel." Ariel was David's little brother who was eighteen months of age and sitting in his high chair in the breakfast area adjacent to the living room in their house.

David and Ariel's mother had stepped out of the room for a moment to take care of something in another part of the house. Just as Jeremiah stepped over to stand behind Ariel, the young child kicked the breakfast table and pushed his high chair backward with his feet. Jeremiah was right there to catch him in the nick of time and keep him from falling and hitting his head on their hard tile floor in that room.

I asked Jeremiah how he knew the voice he heard was the Lord. He answered me, "I thought for a second, Dad, and said, 'What I heard was not a selfish thought.' So I just acted on it and went right away and stood behind Ariel." Wow! This was my seven-year-old son learning to follow God's voice. We need to learn a lesson about following the voice of the Lord from my seven-year-old son: If the thought, leading, or prompting you are sensing from the Lord is not a selfish thought, act on it. Go for it. Lives will be saved, blessed, and healed, just as Ariel's life was spared from certain harm that day by a child following God's voice.

One of the best ways to develop sensitivity to the Lord's voice is learning to follow His leading in operating in the gifts of the Spirit. In the following three chapters I share with you what the Lord has shown me regarding the primary flows of the Spirit. Once you understand the predominant ways the Holy Spirit moves and flows through our lives, you will grow and mature in recognizing His voice clearly and accurately.

Chapter 8

THE FLOW OF LOVE

My wife and I served for more than twenty-seven years in pastoral ministry. During that period of time we pastored two churches—one in South Texas for three years and one in North Texas for twenty-four years. In each of these churches it became a great passion of mine to train our church members to operate in the gifts of the Spirit with confidence.

One of the best ways I discovered to activate people in the gifts was to teach them the primary flows of the Spirit. Jesus taught His disciples the Holy Spirit would flow out of their innermost being.

> *On the last day, that great day of the feast, Jesus stood and cried out, saying, "If anyone thirsts, let him come to Me and drink. He who believes in Me, as the Scripture has said, out of his heart will flow rivers of living*

> *water." But this He spoke concerning the Spirit, whom those believing in Him would receive...* (John 7:37-39).

Jesus described the work of the Spirit in salvation as a *"well of water springing up into everlasting life"* in John 4:14 (KJV). But here in John 7 He describes another dimension of being filled with the Spirit as *"rivers of living water"* that would flow out of us. The well in us benefits us. The rivers of living water flowing out of us benefits others.

A companion verse to this passage in John 7 is found in Ezekiel 47:

> *And it shall be that every living thing that moves, wherever the rivers go, will live...for they will be healed, and everything will live wherever the river goes* (Ezekiel 47:9).

Wow! What a powerful revelation and verse. Wherever the river from within us is flowing, healing and life are the results. In order to release God's healing power and move in the gifts of the Spirit, we must learn to recognize and follow the flow of God's Spirit in us.

The Holy Spirit in John 7:37-39 and Ezekiel 47:9 is likened to water. Water flows from high elevations to lower elevations. The Holy Spirit was sent from Heaven flowing into the earth, seeking out the low places of human suffering, weakness, and bondage. He seeks out those who are lost, hurting, and in darkness. You and I are now the channels (high elevations) He flows from to lift others up. Each of us in Christ are seated together with Him in heavenly places, as revealed in Ephesians 2:6. That doesn't make us more valuable or better than others we are ministering to. It just gives us the privilege and responsibility to be the channels He flows through to lift up others from their low spiritual condition to their full new creation potential in Christ.

I want you to notice something from Peter's message to the multitude on the day of Pentecost. He is quoting a passage from the book of Joel when he says:

> *And it shall come to pass in the last days, says God, that I will pour out of My Spirit on all flesh; your sons and daughters shall prophesy [move out in the gifts], your young men shall see visions, your old men shall dream dreams* (Acts 2:17).

Here in this verse Peter says in the last days God will *pour out of* His Spirit on all flesh. Yet in Joel 2:28, the same verse Peter was quoting from, it says, *"I will pour out My Spirit on all flesh...."* In Joel He said in the last days He would *pour out* His Spirit on all flesh. In the book of Acts, He said in the last days He would *pour out of* His Spirit on all flesh. Can you see the distinction?

In the Old Testament the Holy Spirit did not dwell in men. In the New Testament we have the Holy Spirit abiding in all believers. We are now the vessels He *pours out of* to bless and help hurting people. The Holy Spirit indeed came to bless us, but also to *flow out of us* to touch and bless a hurting world that doesn't know God as a good God who loves them unconditionally.

Three Primary Flows of the Spirit

It is certainly possible to quench the Spirit and stop the flow of the rivers of living water God desires to pour out of us to minister to others. This is caused by us failing to recognize and cooperate with the various flows of the Spirit He is desiring to pour out of us to hurting and broken people. There are three primary flows of the Spirit. If we will recognize each of these and cooperate with the Spirit when He is moving through us in this way, the gifts will flow freely through our lives.

The first flow of the Spirit we need to learn to recognize and follow is *the flow of love.*

> *Now hope does not disappoint, because the love of God has been poured out in our hearts by the Holy Spirit who was given to us* (Romans 5:5).

The first flow of the Spirit is the flow of love that is poured out by the Holy Spirit in our hearts in compassion toward others. Each person reading this who is born again can recognize this major flow of the Spirit. Have you ever had the compassion of the Lord rise up in you toward someone who is hurting or in need? Sure you have. This has happened to all of us. The question is, what did you do with that? More importantly, what will you do with that in the future? The apostle Paul provides us with the answer in the following verse:

> *Pursue love, and desire spiritual gifts...* (1 Corinthians 14:1).

Pursuing love and flowing with the compassion the Spirit is moving through you toward others is the best way to release the spiritual gifts in you. This verse and principle is so clear. The way we release the gifts in us is to follow the flow of love that moves us to minister to others. This is exactly how Jesus released the gifts through His own ministry.

> *And when Jesus went out He saw a great multitude; and He was moved with compassion for them, and healed their sick* (Matthew 14:14).

Jesus understood that by following love, the power of God would be released through Him. The results were multitudes healed. We too need to understand that following love and compassion flowing out of us toward someone will release God's power to meet their needs.

Several years ago, a man I'll call Jeff began attending our church in Decatur, Texas, for a period of time. He had been in prison, had come to the Lord, and was being discipled by a group of men in our church. He was hungry for the Word, very teachable, and was growing in his walk with the Lord. As I was driving through town late one afternoon I realized I was very close to the house where Jeff was living. I felt the prompting of the Lord to stop by and see him.

Jeff was living with his grandmother and happened to be home that day. He invited me in and we sat down in the living room and were talking about the things of the Lord and what God had been showing him from the Word. I wasn't there ten minutes before I noticed an elderly woman who was bent over and walking very slowly from their kitchen into another room in their house. The compassion of the Lord began to flow through me toward her to the point I could no longer focus on my discussion with Jeff.

I asked Jeff who this woman was and he told me it was his aunt Grace. I asked him what was wrong with her. He said she had been that way for a while, but it had gotten worse lately and she was in a lot of pain. He said he thought it had to do with rheumatoid arthritis and the doctors had not been able to help her much. I asked him if he would introduce me to her and if he thought it would be okay to pray for her. He responded, "Sure, Pastor Greg, but she is Fundamental Baptist and I don't know if she believes in that healing business too much."

I let him know God loves people from all denominations and wants to relieve them from their pain and heal them. Jeff introduced me to his aunt and told her I was "his preacher." She told me Jeff had talked a lot about me and she appreciated what our church was doing for him. I told her I noticed she seemed to be in a lot of pain as she walked and asked her if I could pray for her.

Act on Compassion

She said, "Sure sonny, a little prayer won't hurt anyone." At this time the compassion of the Lord was flowing so strongly through me toward her I don't even remember all that I prayed. I just know that when I began to pray for her, I held one of her hands and put my other hand on her back and said, "In Jesus' name, pain leave her." She instantly stood straight up and said, "Whoa! That was a mighty powerful prayer, sonny." It was like electricity was flowing through me to her.

I believe a gift of healing was released through me that day to Jeff's aunt, Grace. She had been bent over at the waist and now she was standing straight up and moving around, lifting her hands and praising the Lord the pain was gone. Praise God! When the compassion and love of God is flowing through us and we follow that flow, the gifts of the Spirit and healing power of God will be released through us. Everywhere the river of God's Spirit in us flows, healing and life will manifest!

Apostle Paul learned how to follow this flow of love as witnessed by his statement in the following verse:

The love of Christ compels us... (2 Corinthians 5:14).

God's love in Paul compelled him, controlled him, and moved him. If we will let His love move us, the power of God and gifts of the Spirit will be released through our lives. As we learn to follow that flow of love and compassion in us, God will truly *pour out of His Spirit* through us on everyone that compassion flows to.

I know this principle may not be new to you. Each of us has had experiences where God's compassion is flowing through us toward others. My encouragement to you is simply to act on the compassion that is moving in you toward others. Pray for them, call them, or reach out to them in some way and watch God manifest Himself and His gifts through you!

> *But earnestly desire the best gifts. And yet I show you a more excellent way* (1 Corinthians 12:31).

This statement by Paul to the Corinthian church is just prior to his description of love in First Corinthians chapter 13. In context, what he was saying by this statement was the more excellent way to see the gifts operate than just desiring them is to follow the flow of love. Which gifts are the best gifts? The ones needed most at the time. The best way to see the best gifts operate in your life is by following the flow of love shed abroad in your heart by the Holy Spirit!

Chapter 9

THE FLOW OF LIGHT

IN THE LAST CHAPTER WE SAW THAT JESUS SAID OUT OF OUR innermost being would flow rivers of living water. He was speaking of the Spirit flowing through us in John 7:37-39. Then in Ezekiel 47:9 we saw that everywhere the river goes healing and life are the result. When we learn to recognize and follow the various flows of the Spirit, we will see more healing, life, and power manifest through our lives and ministry.

There are three primary flows of the Spirit I have seen in the Word and experienced in my own life and ministry. That is not to say there are no other dimensions or flows of the Spirit available to us. But understanding and yielding to the three flows of the Spirit I will share with you in this book will definitely equip and activate you to operate in the gifts with confidence!

In the last chapter I shared with you about the flow of love. I cannot emphasize strongly enough the importance of following the flow of compassion whenever it rises up within you toward others. As you practice following the flow of love, your confidence in hearing God's voice and operating in the gifts will improve dramatically. In this chapter I share with you the next primary flow of the Spirit—*the flow of light.*

> *...God is light and in Him is no darkness at all. But if we walk in the light as He is in the light, we have **fellowship** with one another...* (1 John 1:5,7).

A key word to understand in this passage of Scripture is the word "fellowship." The Greek definition of this word is very interesting. It means sharing, communion, making a contribution or distribution. If we include that definition in the context of these verses, we understand when we walk in the light that God gives us we can share with someone and make a contribution or distribution of something significant and spiritual to them. That certainly lines up with the following companion verses:

> *For I long to see you, that I may impart to you some spiritual gift, so that you may be established* (Romans 1:11).

> *But the manifestation of the Spirit is given to each one for the profit of all* (1 Corinthians 12:7).

I have discovered in my walk with the Lord the more responsive I am to the smallest prompting, leading, or "light" I receive from the Lord, the more the gifts operate through me and the greater blessing I am to others. Bobby Crow is a missionary in Mexico and good friend of mine. One of his famous quotes is, *"The Holy Spirit works best where He finds the least resistance."* I agree with Bobby's statement wholeheartedly.

Revelation and Illumination

When I am talking about the flow of light, I am speaking of revelation or illumination that lines up with God's Word. This light, revelation, or illumination can come to us in many ways. It can come to us while we are reading the Word.

> *Your word is a lamp to my feet and a light to my path* (Psalm 119:105).

There have been numerous times I have simply been reading the Bible in my daily devotions and the Lord illuminated or highlighted a specific verse to me I knew I was to act upon. Each time I have acted on the light He revealed to me from His Word, people have been blessed, I have been blessed, and the gifts of the Spirit have been available to operate through me. After all, doesn't His Word tell us He will work with us confirming His Word with signs following? (See Mark 16:20.)

This flow of light can also come to us by a thought, impression, or inward desire. Before you act on the thought, impression, or inward desire, you will want take time to check it out and make sure it lines up with the written Word. You will also want to think about how this will affect others. In some cases, it will be necessary to receive godly counsel from mature leaders in the church if you have any questions about the direction you have received.

Most of the time light comes to us in one of these three forms— it is not something we need to take a long time to pray and seek God about. The reason for this is what we received does not violate the Word and is intended to bless and minister to others. In these cases, we don't need to allow our brain to take over. Just go for it. Act on the thought, impression, or inward desire you have and then evaluate the result.

I was ministering in a church in the southern part of Texas several years ago and invited people to come forward for healing after my message. While I was praying for people who had responded to my invitation, I started to pray for a young woman when I heard the Lord say, "Don't lay hands on her for healing yet." I immediately pulled my hands back and then asked the question, "Lord, what do You want me to say to her or do for her?" A thought then came to me, "Ask her about her relationship with her dad before you pray for her." I wasn't sure that was the Lord but I thought to myself, *What do I have to lose? The Lord told me not to lay hands on her for healing yet so I might as well follow up on this subsequent thought that came to me.*

When I asked her to tell me about her relationship with her dad she broke down in tears, bent over and began sobbing. It was heart-wrenching to see her so broken in response to my question about her father. As soon as she was able, she shared with me about the abusive relationship she had experienced from her father. Until that day she had not been able to forgive him and that was giving place to the enemy to afflict her emotions with torment and her body with severe pain.

As a result of the question I asked her about her relationship with her dad, for the very first time she saw the connection between the unforgiveness she had toward her father and the torment and pain she was experiencing in her mind and body. She immediately repented before the Lord and forgave her dad. Then I laid hands on her and commanded the torment to leave her mind and the pain to leave her body in Jesus' name. She was instantly healed and set free and started weeping and rejoicing. But this time her tears were tears of joy! All of this came from me simply responding to the light the Lord brought to my mind in the form of a thought.

Responding to the Light

The flow of light can also come through a message you hear someone teach or preach or a prophetic word someone speaks to you. Regarding prophetic words, you need to know you are not obligated to act on every word someone gives you. You need to take time and pray over it, make sure it lines up with the written Word and is confirmed in your heart. No prophetic word ever stands alone or is the whole message.

> *For we know in part, and we prophesy in part* (1 Corinthians 13:9).

Notice in this verse Paul says when we prophesy we only prophesy in part. In other words, no prophecy is ever the entire message God wants to speak to us. Many times it is just the ignitor that leads us into searching God's mind and will through His Word and prayer in that area. I share much more about the flow of light that comes through prophecy later in this book in the chapter entitled, "How to Judge a Prophetic Word." I know that chapter will be a blessing to you.

Another way the flow of light can come to us is through visions or dreams. Acts chapter 10 records that Peter had the same vision three times on a housetop at Simon the tanner's house, and as a result, Cornelius and his entire household were saved. Acts chapter 16 reveals the vision Paul received after the Spirit forbade him to go to Asia and Bithynia to preach the gospel:

> *And a vision appeared to Paul in the night. A man of Macedonia stood and pleaded with him, saying, "Come over to Macedonia and help us." Now after he had seen the vision, immediately we sought to go to Macedonia,*

*concluding that the Lord had called us to preach the gospel
to them* (Acts 16:9-10).

The result of Paul and Silas following this vision was the door
of the gospel was opened to the continent of Europe and the church
was established there in many cities. A vision is something you
see in your mind's eye from the Lord while you are awake. For a
brief time, it seems like your physical senses are suspended and
what you see and hear in that vision seem more real than your
immediate surroundings.

A dream is something you see and/or hear from the Lord while
you are sleeping. The wise men were warned in a dream not to
return to Herod after they had found young Jesus (Matthew 2:12).
Joseph was subsequently warned in a dream to take his family to
Egypt to escape Herod's plan to kill all young male children in the
region from two years old and younger (Matthew 2:13). Spiritual
dreams are still available for us today as the following verse reveals:

*And it shall come to pass in the last days, says God,
that I will pour out of My Spirit on all flesh; your sons
and daughters shall prophesy, your young men shall see
visions, your old men shall dream dreams* (Acts 2:17).

Spiritual Dreams

Though I have had many dreams in my life, very few of them have
proven to be of a spiritual nature. My wife, on the other hand, has
had a number of dreams that proved to be from the Lord. One
dream she had I remember very clearly. I had set up a meeting with
an individual who needed to be confronted about his actions and
some unwarranted accusations against me and our church. I had an
uneasy feeling about this meeting; two nights before it was scheduled, Janice had a dream. In the dream she saw the individual I was

scheduled to meet with sitting in a courtroom playing a recording of our meeting before a judge.

When she woke up the next morning, she told me about her dream and it confirmed the uneasy feeling I was having about this meeting. The Lord was showing us the plans this individual had to bait me into saying something he could use against me and our church in court. This could have cost us a lot of unnecessary heartache, time, and money. I cancelled that meeting and haven't heard from this person since. Praise God for the light that can come to us through dreams.

Sometimes the flow of light comes through what we perceive to be the Spirit speaking directly to our spirit. One example of this is when the Holy Spirit told Peter to go with the men from Cornelius' household, doubting nothing because He had sent them to him (Acts 11:12). Another example is found in the following verses:

> *As they ministered to the Lord and fasted, the Holy Spirit said, "Now separate to Me Barnabas and Saul for the work to which I have called them." Then, having fasted and prayed, and laid hands on them, they sent them away (Acts 13:2-3).*

This passage does not tell us how the Spirit spoke to them. But it is certain that through whomever this message came it bore witness to all because they acted on what they perceived the Spirit had spoken to them.

Show Yourself to Me

Several years ago, I was driving through the southwest part of Houston, Texas, while taking care of some business. It was about four o'clock in the afternoon and the traffic was heavy. I turned off one of the main roads to a street I knew was a shortcut to my destination with less traffic. As I made the right turn onto this side street, I noticed a large set of apartments on the left side of the street and a grassy hill in front of a creek on the right side of the street. On top of this small grassy knoll was a young man with long hair who was on one knee staring up into the sky with one of his arms extended upward.

My first thought was, *There's a hippie spaced out on drugs.* As I passed him by and started to turn my radio on to hear the traffic reports, I heard the Spirit speak to my spirit, "Go join yourself to that man." My first response to that voice was, "Lord, You know I am not in the drug culture and I don't have a voice or ministry to hippies." I had only been filled with the Spirit for a couple of years at this time and was still new in recognizing and following the Lord's voice.

As I continued driving down this side street, I heard His voice again and this time a bit stronger, "Go join yourself to that man." Again I attempted to shrug off this voice and was now over a block away when I heard Him speak to me stronger and louder, "I said, 'Go join yourself to that man!'" I finally surrendered, turned my van around, drove back to where I had seen this young man and pulled into the apartment parking lot directly across from that grassy hill. As I was turning my van around I thought to myself, *What do I have to lose? If I try to minister to this young man and he doesn't receive it, I don't know him and haven't seen him before so nothing lost, nothing gained.*

I walked across the street and walked right up to this man. I extended my right hand to him, introduced myself, and said, "The Lord impressed me to stop, come tell you He loves you and has a really good plan for your life." He stared at me with a look like, "Please leave me alone and get out of my space." When he glared at me without saying anything for about ten seconds I thought, *I told You, Lord, I don't have a ministry to hippies.*

All of a sudden, this word came to me while he was glaring at me, "Tell him I know he lost his job last week, he just had his car repossessed last night, and was served an eviction notice from his apartment across the street this morning." I thought, *Well, what do I have to lose? I have come this far. I might as well go all the way.* Then I told him the word the Lord gave me for him. He began to tremble and big tears started streaming down his face. He asked me, "How did you know those things? I was working construction and fell off a roof and had to go to the hospital for them to do surgery on my knee."

He then showed me the bandage on his left knee through the hole in his jeans, before holes in jeans were in style. He went on to tell me it happened to him just like I said. He lost his job last week right after he was released from the hospital. He had his car repossessed last night, and received an eviction notice from his apartment that morning. He then told me, "After all that happened and I had run out of money and food, I walked over to this grassy hill and looked up to the sky and said, 'God, if You are real, show Yourself to me or I'm going to take my life.' Then you walked up to me about three minutes later and told me God knew what I was going through. What should I do?"

I asked him his name and he said, "Billy." Of course, I led Billy to the Lord, then invited him to my house for dinner. We later took him to our church and he was filled with the Spirit. We gave him our car and he was able to get a new job and find a new place to live. His life was saved spirit, soul, and body and he found a brand-new life. All of this happened because of the flow of light that came to me that day!

There are many more Billys out there waiting for someone to bring them some good news, love, and encouragement. Yet we don't know who they are or where they are. But the Spirit in us does and He will lead us by the flow of light He gives us. All He needs you and I to do is to follow the light.

The flow of light comes in many forms and many ways. I have shared a few of these ways with you. In my encounter with Jeff's aunt, Grace, the flow of love came first and afterward there was light. With Billy, the flow of light came first. Then came compassion. I had zero compassion flowing toward Billy initially. But after I heard his story, great compassion flowed through me toward him to help him receive the Lord, to understand how valuable and loved he was, and to get hm back on his feet financially.

When we learn to follow the flow of love and the flow of light, His life and power will be released in and through our lives. People will be saved, healed, set free, and the gifts will flow through us freely!

Chapter 10

THE FLOW OF LIFE

I HAVE BEEN SHARING WITH YOU FOR THE LAST TWO CHAPTERS about the primary flows of the Spirit. When we understand the primary ways the Spirit moves through us and cooperate with Him, we will experience a radical increase of the supernatural in our lives. That has certainly been the case in my own life and ministry. This is my desire and, more importantly, God's desire for you.

The first two of the three primary flows of the Spirit are the *flow of love* and the *flow of light*. I want to share with you now about the *flow of life*. This flow of the Spirit is not as common as the first two. But it has occurred a number of times in my own ministry and many times has resulted in healings and miracles. Early on I was not aware of it and did not know how to cooperate with it. Once I understood it and yielded to it, I saw much greater results in the release of the gifts of the Spirit through my life.

> *...He who raised Christ from the dead will also give life to your mortal bodies through His Spirit who dwells in you* (Romans 8:11).

> *...that the life of Jesus also may be manifested in our mortal flesh* (2 Corinthians 4:11).

These two verses of Scripture are the foundation for our understanding of the flow of life. In Romans 8 in the King James version it says the Spirit will "quicken" or make alive, give life to our mortal bodies. And then in Second Corinthians 4 it says the life of Jesus might be manifest in our mortal flesh. This flow of life involves the tangible presence of Jesus and the anointing of His Spirit that produces divine quickening in our mortal bodies.

Falling Under the Spirit's Power

We know God is present in us and with us at all times. But there are times when His tangible presence is manifest so strongly that even our mortal bodies can feel it, sense it, and be impacted by it. Have you ever known someone who has experienced "falling under the power of the Spirit"? Have you ever had that experience? Why is it in those situations that people fall? Because they cannot stand. What is the Scripture reference and basis for this? There are several references for this experience of an individual's flesh giving way to the Spirit. I will share three of these with you.

> *...then the house was filled with a cloud, even the house of the Lord; so that **the priests could not stand** to minister by reason of the cloud: for the glory of the Lord had filled the house of God* (2 Chronicles 5:13-14 KJV).

> *Jesus therefore, knowing all things that would come upon Him, went forward and said to them, "Whom are you*

*seeking?" They answered Him, "Jesus of Nazareth." Jesus said to them, "I am He" …Now when He said to them, "I am He," **they** drew back and **fell** to the ground* (John 18:4-6).

*As he journeyed he came near Damascus, and suddenly a light shone around him from heaven. Then **he fell** to the earth, and heard a voice saying to him, "Saul, Saul, why are you persecuting Me?"* (Acts 9:3-4)

Here are three cases where the presence of God was so strong individuals could not stand. The priests could not stand to minister because of the glory of God. The soldiers fell backward to the ground because of the presence and words of Jesus. And Saul (Paul) fell to the ground when a light shined from Heaven and he heard the voice of Jesus. There is a manifest presence of Jesus I call the flow of life that will have an effect on your physical body.

When we understand the purpose of that tangible presence of God and cooperate with it, life will be the result. With the priests there was a focus on the presence of God. With the soldiers it resulted in the fear of the Lord that most likely caused them to spare the lives of Jesus' disciples and let them go. With Saul, it caused him to get saved. I shared with you earlier about my daughter-in-law, Jessica, who fell out under the power of the Spirit when Dave Duell prayed for her. The result of that was she was healed of scar tissue and able to conceive and give us three more grandchildren!

When that tangible presence and anointing—the flow of life—manifests in some way in your life, the Bible says the anointing in you will teach you.

But the anointing which you have received from Him abides in you, and you do not need that anyone teach you; but as the same anointing teaches you concerning all things, and is true, and is not a lie, and just as it has taught you, you will abide in Him (1 John 2:27).

His anointing is in you to teach you about all things, including the purpose of these times of His manifest presence and flow of life in your life. If you will simply take time to pray in the Spirit and seek Him, He will show why He has manifested Himself in this fashion. And He will show you how to respond to Him that His life will manifest in your life.

Cooperating with the Flow of Life

The first year I served as pastor of our church in Decatur, Texas, I learned an important lesson about cooperating with the flow of life. One Wednesday evening we had a service with about fifty to sixty people present. During the worship service I felt heat and a tingling in my left hand. I had been lifting my hands in worship, so I pulled my left arm down, thinking my arm or hand had somehow had the blood cut off to it and that was producing the tingling feeling.

But that was not what was causing the heat and tingling in my hand. As we worshiped it got stronger. I remembered hearing Kenneth Hagin share that sometimes he could feel a burning sensation in his hands. He said whenever that happened he learned to cooperate with the Spirit and call for people who needed healing right away. He said that anointing in his hands released the gifts of healings to many people, especially those with growths and goiters.

As we continued to worship that night, I began to pray quietly in the Spirit, knowing I had the Holy Spirit and His anointing in me and He would teach me what to do with this heat and tingling in my left hand. As I continued to pray in the Spirit and worship, it became clear to me He had already given me a reference point in

Kenneth Hagin what to do when I have a strong heat or sensation in my hands. This was the first time I had experienced this, and I knew I needed to call people forward who needed healing.

As soon as we finished worship, I took the mic and asked if anyone needed prayer for healing. Several people came forward. But there was a man I had not noticed before the service who was seated at the back of the church and had come in late. His name was Bill and he had just been released from the hospital after experiencing a heart attack. He still had the hospital tag around his wrist.

I knew I was supposed to lay my left hand on him and God would heal him. When I did, it felt like electricity flowing through my left hand to him and he fell out under the power of the Spirit. He stayed down for several minutes; when he got up he was lifting his hands, praising God, and doing a little dance because he said he felt 100 percent better. Then he told us the story of his recent heart attack, his stay in the hospital, and how the Lord told him to come to our service that night and he would receive a new heart.

Heat and Tingling

The flow of life manifested through heat and tingling in my left hand that night and it resulted in Bill receiving a new heart. Praise God! This has happened a number of times since that service where one or both of my hands are burning or tingling and it doesn't go away until I get my hands on someone who is sick. This flow of life works in conjunction with the gifts of healings and working of miracles. And it especially works through me in people who have heart problems.

Don't get me wrong. I will pray for anyone. But I have learned this flow of life that manifests through heat and tingling in my hands will release one of the gifts of healing for anyone who has a bad heart. With Brother Hagin it was especially for people who had growths or goiters. I will still lay hands on anyone who needs healing when that flow of life is at work in my hands. But I have seen more results with hearts being healed than anything else when this occurs.

There is one important thing I need to mention here. It is very easy for people to receive healing through the gifts of the Spirit. But they cannot maintain their healing through the gifts of the Spirit. You stay healed by your faith in the Word and the finished work of the cross! I cannot pray the flow of life into manifestation to have my hands burn and tingle whenever I want or whenever I know someone needs healing for their heart. But I can speak the Word to them, lay hands on them in faith, and know the Lord will still confirm His Word with signs following.

I want to share one additional manifestation of the flow of life you may experience from time to time. This is a burning or bubbling forth of the Spirit within that will move us to prophesy, preach, teach, or respond to some invitation or command from the Lord.

> *My heart was hot within me, while I was musing the fire burned; then I spoke with my tongue* (Psalm 39:3).

> *Then I said, "I will not make mention of Him, nor speak anymore in His name." But His Word was in my heart like a burning fire shut up in my bones; I was weary of holding it back, and I could not* (Jeremiah 20:9).

I have experienced this a number of times where the passion and fire within me to prophesy, preach, or teach a message was so strong it seemed like I would burst on the inside. It seemed as though I could not control it. Yet I know I can because the Word says the spirits of the prophets are subject to the prophets; see First Corinthians 14:32. In other words, we do have control over ourselves and what we say or don't say.

A Word from God

A few years ago at an Andrew Wommack ministers' conference, this kind of flow of life was manifesting within me. During the worship time in one of the night services I knew I had a word for the pastors there regarding fresh encounters with the Living God. I knew I needed to share this with them and then have several of us lay hands on them and minister to them. It was bubbling up from my spirit and my heart was hot within me. It was like a fire burning in my bones as Jeremiah said. I prayed in the Spirit for a short time and then told the Lord, "Lord, this is not my service. If You want me to share this, speak to Andrew or someone in charge and I will respond."

As soon as I spoke that prayer out, Charlie LeBlanc, the worship leader for that conference said, "The Lord has shown me someone has a word for the pastors and ministers here tonight." As soon as Charlie shared what the Lord had shown him, I knew that was me. I jumped up on the stage immediately and shared that word. And we had a powerful move of God among the pastors and ministers present as we laid hands on them, blessed them, and prayed for them.

The point is, whenever this kind of flow of life is moving in you, take time to pray over it and seek God about how and where you are to deliver the word He has burdened your heart with sharing. As you pray in the Spirit, He will show you where, how, and with whom to share what your heart is burning within you to share.

One final point I want to address in the context of the flow of life is "empathy pains." I have heard some people testify how they received certain pains in their body to let them know to pray for someone who had the same pain. This is like a word of knowledge that supposedly comes to them in the form of a pain. I am not going to split hairs or debate with anyone on this point, but I don't believe this is part of the flow of life.

If you know of someone who was healed through someone else receiving a similar pain to let them know to pray for them, praise God. As long as their testimony includes their "empathy pain" left too, I am not going to argue with you about it. My struggle with this is on a biblical basis found in Isaiah 53.

> *Surely He has borne our griefs [sicknesses] and carried our sorrows [pains]...* (Isaiah 53:4).

Since Jesus carried our pains for us, I have difficulty believing He will give us pains to help relieve pain in others. That seems very counterproductive to me. What I have experienced and see in the Word is a sense that someone is experiencing pain in a particular area that produces great empathy and compassion in me for what they are going through. The writer of Hebrews puts it like this:

> *For we have not an high priest which cannot be touched with the feeling of our infirmities...* (Hebrews 4:15 KJV).

I know the Lord is touched with what touches us and impacts us. Allowing ourselves to be touched by the tenderness of the Good Shepherd toward hurting people will open us up to receive words of wisdom and words of knowledge regarding their condition and release healing to them. I am convinced this is more a work of the flow of love than the flow of life.

The bottom line—God is after people being well, free from bondage, and free from pain. And He has equipped you and me to be healing and delivering agents of His by recognizing and following the three primary flows of the Spirit: the flow of love, the flow of light, and the flow of life.

Chapter 11

BECOME FAMILIAR WITH THE GIFTS

ONE OF THE PRIMARY PURPOSES OF THIS BOOK IS TO HELP YOU develop confidence in operating in the gifts and flowing in the supernatural. An essential principle in accomplishing that goal is knowing what each of the gifts of the Spirit are and how they work. There are entire books devoted to this topic alone. I will not attempt to provide you a comprehensive study of the gifts in this one chapter. My goal is to give you a clear definition of each gift and at least one example of how it operates. Once you are familiar with each gift, you will become a greater candidate for the Holy Spirit to use you in the supernatural power of God. Let's look at these gifts:

> *For to one is given the **word of wisdom** through the Spirit, to another the **word of knowledge** through the*

*same Spirit, to another **faith** by the same Spirit, to another gifts of **healings** by the same Spirit, to another the working of **miracles**, to another **prophecy**, to another **discerning** of spirits, to another different kinds of **tongues**, to another the **interpretation of tongues*** (1 Corinthians 12:8-10).

There are nine gifts of the Spirit listed here and there are three categories of these gifts. There are *three revelation gifts:* the word of wisdom, the word of knowledge, and discerning of spirits. There are *three power gifts:* faith, gifts of healings, and the working of miracles. There are *three vocal gifts:* prophecy, different kinds of tongues, and the interpretation of tongues. I will define and explain these gifts in this order because it has helped me to study and think about them in that way.

Before I start, I want to share a disclaimer with you. I don't think I am the final authority on understanding the gifts of the Spirit. Nor do I believe the definitions I provide you are all comprehensive. However, I have studied about the gifts for over forty years. I have read entire books devoted to teaching on the gifts of the Spirit from Howard Carter, Lester Sumrall, John Osteen, Kenneth Hagin, Norvel Hayes, Ron Smith, and others. I have also experienced and observed the operation of each gift through my ministry and the ministry of many contemporary ministries.

I have had a passion for more than forty years to see the gifts operate in the church today like we read throughout the Bible, especially in the gospels and the book of Acts. The following definitions of the gifts are based on what I have seen in the Word, have studied from other seasoned and respected Christian leaders, and observed in operation either through my ministry or the ministry of others.

Revelation Gifts

The word of wisdom: A word of revelation in the mind of God of what is going to take place in the future or how to resolve a difficult situation

Many times what people believe is a prophetic word is actually a word of wisdom. This is the revelation gift that is foretelling the future. In First Kings 17:1, God told Elijah to go to King Ahab and tell him it would not rain except at his word, and it did not rain for more than three years. That was a word of wisdom.

What the angel of the Lord spoke to Paul and he subsequently shared with the men on the ship with him in the middle of a great storm was a word of wisdom:

> *And now I urge you to take heart, for there will be no loss of life among you, but only of the ship. For there stood by me this night an angel of the God to whom I belong and whom I serve, saying, "Do not be afraid, Paul; you must be brought before Caesar; and indeed God has granted you all those who sail with you." Therefore take heart, men, for I believe God that it will be just as it was told me* (Acts 27:22-25).

Ron Smith was a prophet to the church I pastored in Decatur, Texas. He came at least annually to our church for twenty-four years. One year he came and said, "Expand your nursery, Pastor Greg. God is giving this church many new babies." In one year's time we had ten new babies in our nursery! Five of them were from present church members and five came from new members God sent in. This was a word of wisdom. This gift will establish people in their hope and trust in God, create a spirit of expectation in the church, and realization God is present with us.

> **The word of knowledge:** Supernatural revelation by the Holy Spirit of certain facts in the mind of God relating to the past or present

This gift will reveal to us something specific that is happening in an individual's life at the present time and/or what they have experienced in the past. This gift does not reveal to you everything about an individual. It is a *word* of knowledge, not a book. These gifts do not make us mind readers. The purpose of this gift is to help people receive an understanding of God's love and care for them, peace, freedom, and healing. First Samuel 9:3 tells us that Saul and a servant were sent by his father to look for their lost donkeys. After Saul finds Samuel and Samuel anoints Saul as king, Samuel shares this word with Saul about the lost donkeys:

> *When you have departed from me today, you will find two men by Rachel's tomb in the territory of Benjamin at Zelzah; and they will say to you, "The donkeys which you went to look for have been found. And now your father has ceased caring about the donkeys and is worrying about you"…* (1 Samuel 10:2).

Samuel gave Saul a word of wisdom about the two men he would meet and then a word of knowledge that his father's donkeys had been found and that his father was worrying about Saul. Jesus gave a word of knowledge to the woman at the well that caused her to recognize Him as the Messiah:

> *Jesus said to her, "Go, call your husband, and come here."*
> *The woman answered and said, "I have no husband."*

Jesus said to her, "You have well said, 'I have no husband,' for you have had five husbands, and the one whom you now have is not your husband; in that you spoke truly" (John 4:16-18).

Jesus' knowledge of her past—*"you have had five husbands"*—and her present—*"the one you now have is not your husband"*—were two specific words of knowledge that brought her to faith in Jesus. When the word of knowledge is operating in the church, it ministers a strong sense of peace, assurance, and security to people. It also helps establish them in their understanding of the love of the Father.

> **Discerning of spirits:** Supernatural ability to see into the spirit realm and recognize what spirits are operating and exercising their influence in people's lives

This is not the gift of suspicion. We need to remind ourselves that flesh and blood human beings are not our enemies. We also need to realize this is not just a gift that sees an evil spirit influencing someone. It is also the ability to see angels at work behind the scenes or the condition of someone's human spirit—whether they are born again or not. One example of this is found in Second Kings chapter 6:

And when the servant of the man of God arose early and went out, there was an army, surrounding the city with horses and chariots. And his servant said to him, "Alas, my master! What shall we do?" So he answered, "Do not fear, for those who are with us are more than those who are with them." And Elisha prayed, and said, "Lord, I pray, open his eyes that he may see." Then the

> *Lord opened the eyes of the young man, and he saw. And behold, the mountain was full of horses and chariots of fire all around Elisha* (2 Kings 6:15-17).

We need to remember this important lesson. It is so easy to slip into a negative mindset and focus more on what the enemy is doing than what God is doing in our lives. The devil is defeated; and if we will keep our eyes on the Lord, He will remind us of His finished work on the cross on our behalf and show us the way out of trouble. There are more with us than with the enemy!

The Lord will use this gift to help us know the spirit an individual is yielding to in order to protect us from making commitments or putting someone in leadership whose motive is selfish ambition or self-promotion.

> *But Peter said to him, "Your money perish with you, because you thought that the gift of God could be purchased with money! You have neither part nor portion in this matter, for your heart is not right in the sight of God. Repent therefore of this your wickedness, and pray God if perhaps the thought of your heart may be forgiven you. For* **I see** *that you are poisoned by bitterness and bound by iniquity* (Acts 8:20-23).

Notice in verse 23 that Peter said to Simon, *"I see that you are poisoned by bitterness."* This was the discerning of spirits in operation in Peter. He saw what Simon had yielded to in his heart. But also notice he confronted Simon by appealing to him to repent. Peter used this gift in a redemptive fashion rather than judgment.

Power Gifts

Faith: Gift of power that totally anchors the soul in God in overwhelming confidence to operate or receive gifts of healings or working of miracles

This gift of faith is not the same thing as faith that comes by hearing the Word of God (Romans 10:17). This is a gift that temporarily removes all doubt and fear from your mind. It almost always works in conjunction with the working of miracles and sometimes with gifts of healings. It is also the gift that is predominantly involved in raising people from the dead. I am convinced this was the gift working in Daniel that allowed him to sleep with his hungry lion friends and not be harmed. I call it the gift that transforms Clark Kent into Superman and the normal Christian into a miracle worker.

When I was in Bible college I would normally spend fifteen to twenty minutes praying in my car before going into my first class. One morning while praying and meditating on the Word before class, I felt an overwhelming sense of confidence come over me. I felt like I was invincible. All doubt, self-consciousness, and fear instantly seemed to be sucked out of my mind. I wondered for a bit what I did to warrant this amazing sense of confidence and victory. All I knew was I wanted to find someone who needed a miracle or healing and watch God do the works of Jesus through me.

As I entered my first class that morning, I sat in the second row. I noticed a man sitting in front of me in his fifties who looked grey and ashen in color. While I was thinking of asking him if I could pray for him, he stood up from his seat, bent over, and fell to the floor. I didn't think twice. I leapt over the table in front of me and laid my hands on him and commanded resurrection life into him and death to leave him. His eyes had rolled back in his head, but as soon as I prayed for him, he came to. Someone called 911, so an ambulance came to take him to the hospital.

But he was fine, awake, and smiling, giving us the "thumbs up" sign as he left. He reported back to us the next day that they ran tests on him at the hospital and he had signs of having a heart attack. But all his vital signs were normal and they released him from the hospital early the next morning! After I prayed for him that morning, all that overwhelming sense of confidence and invincibility left me. Superman turned back into Clark Kent. I wondered if I had done something wrong. What the Lord showed me was that was the gift of faith working through me that day to produce a healing miracle in my fellow student.

Understanding how the gift of faith manifests in me has helped me cooperate with it whenever that gift is needed. I asked the Lord to show me that gift operating in the New Testament. He said it happened when Jesus raised Lazarus from the dead. It also happened in Acts 3 when the man lame from birth was healed. He told me Peter and John had passed by this lame man many days, and he was in the same condition as the day before. But this day something was different. The "something different" was the gift of faith. The Lord told me to look at verse 4 where it says, *"And fixing his eyes on him, with John, Peter said, 'Look at us.'"*

The Lord showed me the *"fixing his eyes"* on this lame man indicated the complete confidence and focus the gift of faith gave to Peter at that moment. And of course this lame man leapt, walked, and praised God. The gift of faith in Peter produced a miracle in this man. And the gift of faith working through you will produce miracles in others.

> **Gifts of healings:** Supernatural power to deliver the
> sick and destroy the works of satan in the human
> body

This gift many times works in conjunction with the word of wisdom, the word of knowledge, or the gift of faith. Naaman the leper was healed by a combination of the word of wisdom and a gift of healing from the prophet Elisha:

> *And Elisha sent a messenger to him [Naaman], saying,*
> *"Go and wash in the Jordan seven times, and your flesh*
> *shall be restored to you, and you shall be clean"* (2 Kings
> 5:10).

Jesus operated in the gift of the word of wisdom and the gift of healing together when He told the ten lepers to *"Go, show your-selves to the priests"* (Luke 17:14) and when He told the blind man to *"Go, wash in the pool of Siloam"* (John 9:7). Many healing evangelists operate in the word of knowledge in combination with the gifts of healings. I have observed Kathryn Kuhlman and Benny Hinn call out by the word of knowledge various ailments the Lord was healing and seeing scores of people healed. I have seen many healings through my own ministry through the word of knowledge and then the gifts of healings are released.

Sometimes the Lord assigns a particular gift of healing to a ministry and they will see many people healed in one or two specific kinds of sicknesses or ailments. For example, Acts 8:7 says through Philip's ministry many demon-possessed, paralyzed, and lame were healed. God is not limited and His healing power is available to everyone. But He does have specialists who see more results in par-ticular kinds of sickness and disease than others. Especially when it involves gifts of healings.

> **The working of miracles:** Supernatural intervention into the ordinary course of nature that results in miracles or healings

Jesus performed many miracles. His first miracle was when He turned the water into wine at the wedding at Cana (John 2:11). Another of His miracles was multiplying the loaves and fishes recorded in John chapter 6. Another powerful miracle of His was raising Lazarus from the dead in John chapter 11. Also, the book of Acts is filled with miracles the early church performed, including many miracles of healing and raising people from the dead.

There is an important thing to note about miracles, whether they are done by Jesus or His disciples, including you and me. A miracle usually starts by someone hearing God and they almost always involve others in the process.

> *Therefore He who supplies the Spirit to you and works miracles among you, does He do it by the works of the law, or by the hearing of faith?* (Galatians 3:5)

The Vocal Gifts

> **Prophecy:** Supernatural utterance in a known tongue inspired by the Spirit to build up the church or an individual

When many people hear the word "prophecy," they connect it to either end-time events or the function of the word of wisdom. Though prophecy can contain revelation such as a word of wisdom or word of knowledge, the real function of this gift is described in the following verse:

> *But he who prophesies speaks edification and exhortation and comfort to men* (1 Corinthians 14:3).

The purpose of prophecy is to edify or encourage, exhort or call near to God, and to comfort others. A good example of prophecy is the words Elizabeth spoke over Mary when Mary came to her house after her visitation by the angel Gabriel.

> *And it happened, when Elizabeth heard the greeting of Mary, that the babe leaped in her womb; and Elizabeth was filled with the Holy Spirit. Then she spoke out with a loud voice and said, "Blessed are you among women, and blessed is the fruit of your womb! But why is this granted to me, that the mother of my Lord should come to me? For indeed, as soon as the voice of your greeting sounded in my ears, the babe leaped in my womb for joy. Blessed is she who believed, for there will be a fulfillment of those things which were told her from the Lord"* (Luke 1:41-45).

This prophecy did include revelation that was present—Mary was pregnant with Jesus the Messiah—and future—there will be a fulfillment of these things the Lord told you. But this was certainly a gift of prophecy because of the great confirmation and encouragement it brought to Mary.

> **Different kinds of tongues:** Supernatural utterance in an unknown tongue (unknown to the speaker) intended to be interpreted in a public setting

There are three different levels or uses of tongues according to the Word:

1. *In your personal prayer life* where you are speaking mysteries to God (1 Corinthians 14:2) and edifying yourself (1 Corinthians 14:4). Praying in tongues in your personal prayer life is not required to be interpreted, though it can be from time to time as the Holy Spirit reveals to you what you have been praying. I will share more about the benefits of this use of tongues in a later chapter of this book entitled, "The Benefits of Praying in Tongues."

2. *A message given in church or some public gathering* as a gift of tongues, which when interpreted will edify the church (1 Corinthians 14:13).

3. *A ministry equipped with tongues and interpretation of tongues that is part of the ministry assignment and function* (1 Corinthians 12:28). I shared with you earlier in this book about Mom and Dad Goodwin and Ron and Carolyn Smith who operated ministries that were very fluent in this purpose of tongues. When they would flow in this gift and the gift of interpretation of tongues, it was poetic, artistic, anointed, and very powerful to observe. The impact on those present was always very evident. It drew people's attention on the Lord and what He was saying and doing.

The latter two uses of tongues come under the category of the gift of different kinds of tongues while the first use of tongues does not.

> **Interpretation of tongues:** Supernatural showing forth of what has been said in tongues (not a word-by-word translation)

Paul makes a distinction between the use of tongues in his personal life that are not necessary to be interpreted and tongues given out as a message in church that must be interpreted.

> *I thank my God I speak with tongues more than you all;*
> *yet in the church I would rather speak five words with*
> *my understanding that I may teach others also, than ten*
> *thousand words in a tongue* (1 Corinthians 14:18-19).

This gift of interpretation of tongues is equivalent to prophecy when a message in tongues is given publicly and this gift is used to share the intended meaning of the tongue given out publicly (1 Corinthians 14:5). I will share much more about these vocal gifts in the next chapter "Order in the House."

Chapter 12

ORDER IN THE HOUSE

HAVE YOU EVER BEEN TO A CHURCH SERVICE THAT SEEMED OUT OF control? I am referring to those churches or services where the gifts, manifestations, and demonstrations abound with no restraint. It's like a three-ring circus and there is little explanation of what is happening. But those involved all seem to be having a good time. I have been to a number of services like this. One service in particular we attended while traveling in the Midwest part of the country.

We had heard the founder of this church minister at a conference and thought we would visit his church while in the area on vacation. When we entered, what we observed was a spiritual free-for-all. The worship team was playing one song for an extended period of time. During that time many people were running around the church. Many others were waving banners and flags while either walking or running through the crowd. Several others were dancing throughout the auditorium. Then I observed quite a number of people moving throughout the crowd giving words to different people.

There were prophecies given that we could not hear because they didn't use a microphone, the band was still playing and we were not seated close to them. There was no direction given or explanation of what was going on by the leaders of the service. All of this lasted for over an hour and there was very little time spent by the campus pastor to teach the Word. This is how it was in the church at Corinth that Paul addresses in his first letter to the Corinthians. He told them they came behind in no good gift. They were operating in all the gifts with no restraint or order.

Their highest value was their personal liberty over love. Their priority was the personal freedom to operate in the gifts rather than what was in the best interest of the church. Now don't get me wrong. I would rather have a little wild fire like what I just described than be part of a dead, dry church where I know exactly what is going to happen in every service and no one's life is changed!

We began this spiritual journey of learning how to operate in the gifts of the Spirit and flowing in the supernatural by heeding Paul's instruction to us:

> *Now concerning spiritual gifts, brethren, I do not want*
> *you to be ignorant* (1 Corinthians 12:1).

After declaring this, Paul spends three chapters informing us how to flow in the supernatural and operate the gifts in biblical order. Those three chapters are First Corinthians 12, 13, and 14. The focus of chapter 14 is how to operate the vocal gifts—tongues, interpretation of tongues, and prophecy—in the church in order.

Once we learn to operate these gifts in an orderly way, it sets a pattern for us to release the revelation and power gifts appropriately.

Edification and Order

The two themes of First Corinthians 14 are edification and order. You can find the word "edify" in some form at least six times in this one chapter. The following verses are three examples of this:

> *...that the church may receive edification* (verse 5).

> *...let it be for the edification of the church that you seek to excel [in the operation of the gifts]* (verse 12).

> *...Let all things be done for edification* (verse 26).

Paul's chief concern in the release of the gifts in the church is that the church be edified and not just the individual releasing the gifts. Over the years I have observed many who recently became aware the gifts were available to them. And they became very enamored with this newfound dimension of spiritual endowment. I have even observed some using the gifts as a means to impress others of how sensitive to the Spirit and spiritual they were.

Repeating an important lesson to learn: *You cannot bless those you are trying to impress!* That is about you, not others. Answering the following question will help you determine your motive: "Am I doing this to meet a need in my life or in the lives of others?" Releasing the gifts is primarily for others, not you. Order and peace in the church are the result of people exercising the gifts with the motive to edify others, rather than promoting themselves. The bottom line is we want to temper our zeal to release the gifts with a superior zeal to edify the church. In other words, our love for others has to trump the value of our personal liberty in order for divine order to prevail in a church or ministry.

Understanding this principle is the foundational point of order Paul establishes in this chapter. Another point of order Paul outlines in First Corinthians 14 is tongues by themselves do not edify the church but they do edify the individual. Paul endorses the entire church to be filled with the Spirit and speak with other tongues in their individual devotional life.

> *He who speaks in a tongue edifies himself...* (1 Corinthians 14:4).

> *I wish you all spoke with tongues...* (1 Corinthians 14:5).

Paul also establishes a point of order in the public setting of the church—it is better to prophesy than to speak in tongues unless it is interpreted. Within this point he reveals another key principle to know—tongues that are interpreted are equivalent to prophecy. If this is true, why is there any need for tongues and interpretation of tongues? First, because they are gifts given to us by the Spirit, and all of His gifts are good gifts whether we understand them or not.

Second, it is more of a supernatural demonstration of the Spirit when two people are involved in the release and manifestation of a gift. When one person gives a message in tongues and someone else who had no previous communication with the person releasing that gift interprets it, that is something very supernatural to observe. And it is a greater sign to an unbeliever or uninformed person than just one person releasing a prophecy.

Tongues and Interpretation

Another point of order Paul reveals to us here is if you speak out a message in tongues in a public setting in a church—including a home group or home church—it must be interpreted. And if there is no one to interpret the tongue you give out publicly, you must interpret it. Otherwise the public tongue you released is out of order.

> *Therefore let him who speaks in a tongue pray that he may interpret* (1 Corinthians 14:13).

> *What is the conclusion then? I will pray with the spirit, and I will also pray with the understanding* (1 Corinthians 14:15).

> *But if there is no interpreter, let him keep silent in the church, and let him speak to himself and to God* (1 Corinthians 14:28).

I use these verses to provide leadership for those who release a public message in tongues. In some instances, I have asked the individual who gave that public message in tongues to use their faith to interpret it if no one else does within thirty to sixty seconds. Can we as leaders require an individual to do that? Absolutely! How can we assume to do that? Because of God's Word that requires a public message of tongues to be interpreted.

It is also the responsibility of the pastor, church leader, or small group leader to use their faith to interpret a tongue when one is given publicly and no one else steps out in faith and interprets it. Can we have faith to do that? Again I say, absolutely! When God's Word clearly states a public message in tongues must be interpreted it is the responsibility of either the person giving the tongue or the pastor or leader in charge to interpret it. Of course it is best if church members or small group participants are taught to respond to the Spirit and step out in faith to interpret a public tongue.

If we are going to lead a Spirit-filled church, ministry, or group, the leader must take his or her toddler pants off, put on their big-boy or big-girl pants and make sure the instruction from the Word about operating the gifts is fulfilled. This is another reason why many pastors and churches don't allow the gifts to operate at all in their church services. They are fearful they will have to use their faith to interpret a tongue or direct a service the Spirit is controlling. That is a fearful thing for a leader who is leaning to his or her own understanding and own plan for the service.

I tell students and disciples of mine who are desiring to have a ministry where the Spirit has control and the gifts are in operation, *"The Holy Spirit must be President, not just resident!"* In other words, spiritual leaders must learn the value of yielding to the Spirit when leading a service instead of following a prescribed plan. The writer of Proverbs describes it like this:

> *A man's heart plans his way, but the Lord directs his steps* (Proverbs 16:9).

It's okay for leaders to pray and outline a plan for a church service with the light they have. But when we get into the service, we must lean into the Holy Spirit for any course corrections or specifics that are on His heart we did not receive ahead of time. The Lord delights in us remaining dependent upon Him at all times.

Spirit of Competition

The next thing Paul instructs the church regarding the operation of the gifts is to forbid the competitive interpretation of tongues.

> *If anyone speaks in a tongue, let there be two or at the most three, each in turn, and let one interpret* (1 Corinthians 14:27).

Notice the term Paul uses, *"each in turn."* This is a directive for the orderly operation of tongues and interpretation of tongues. When he states, *"let one interpret,"* he is not limiting the ability and freedom to interpret a public message in tongues to only one person. He is simply stating it is out of order for one person to interpret a message in tongues and then another person stand up after that and declare, "I don't believe that was the accurate interpretation of that tongue. I believe I have the more accurate interpretation."

Paul was forbidding the spirit of competition in the operation of these gifts through this instruction. I have witnessed this very thing a number of times in various church services I was leading. Because I knew this principle each time this happened, I was able to let the person who thought they had a better interpretation know what they believe they have from the Lord is a prophecy and not the interpretation to a tongue that was already interpreted.

Can a leader be so bold to tell someone that? Absolutely, because the Spirit is not going to lead people to violate His Word. And His Word says, in effect, "No competitive interpretations allowed." There have been times someone gave a public message in tongues and another interpreted that I did not sense what was given was the interpretation. In those few cases, I simply state, "I believe what this brother or sister spoke after the tongue was actually a prophecy and someone else has the interpretation to the message in tongues." Then I will ask the people present if someone's spirit was being stirred while the tongue was given to go ahead and speak out the interpretation.

In every case that has happened, someone will almost instantly step out and give the interpretation after my encouragement. And in each case, it was very powerful and lifted the hearts of the people. When I have done that it did not embarrass or hurt the individual who first gave out a message, which turned out to be a prophecy. I encouraged both of them and the person who gave the message in tongues that they were hearing from God. This was certainly a subjective judgment on my part when I did that, but each time it bore good fruit. And we were still able to lead the operation of these precious gifts in an orderly way that prevented competitive interpretation.

Limited Number

Another key point of order Paul shares with us is only two or three messages in tongues, interpretation of tongues, and/or prophecies are allowed at a time in a service.

> *If anyone speaks in a tongue, let there be two or at the most three…* (1 Corinthians 14:27).

> *Let two or three prophets speak, and let the others judge* (1 Corinthians 14:29).

The reason for this instruction is after three messages through the vocal gifts, anything else becomes redundant. And it becomes difficult to remember the first message if there are more than three given. In verse 29 it tells us each prophecy given must be judged. How are we to judge these words given? By the written Word, by the inward witness of the individual who is the recipient of the word, and by spiritual leaders in that church, ministry, or small group. In a subsequent chapter in this book we will cover in detail how to judge a prophetic word.

Another important point of order Paul shares regarding the gifts is, "Do not allow any individual to dominate or *hog the show*." Do you know what I mean by that? Have you ever experienced an individual in a small group or church who attempted to interrupt the leader with their insight or who had a comment to share about everything? These are folks who usually have great hearts but undisciplined mouths. They think more highly of their own opinions and ideas than they ought. I affectionately call them,

"Legends in their own minds." And these folks find their way to every church, ministry, and small group that allow the gifts to operate.

Paul addresses this in the following two verses:

> *But if anything is revealed to another who sits by, let the first keep silent* (1 Corinthians 14:30).

> *And the spirits of the prophets are subject to the prophets* (1 Corinthians 14:32).

The first responsibility to submit to this principle is the individual who is speaking, sharing their comments, or releasing their vocal gift. If they will listen to the Spirit and submit to the pastor or spiritual leader in charge of that service or meeting, they can grow and become a great blessing to others when they share and release the gifts. Yet, in my experience, this does not come easy to individuals who have not had strong, caring leadership in their lives.

Therefore, it is the leader's responsibility to teach these things to the people. The people must be taught that each member has something significant to offer and opportunity will be given for each member of the body to operate in the gifts and share what is on their heart as it is appropriate. There is not just one member who is sensitive to the Spirit, can hear God, and release the gifts.

When a leader observes an individual repeatedly dominating a small group or church service with endless comments or interruptions, it is their responsibility to address this individual. I recommend doing it privately first rather than publicly. I believe it is best to praise publicly and correct privately. Each time I have had to do this I start off by expressing appreciation for the individual's passion for the Word, the gifts, and contribution to the group or church.

Next I appeal to them based on the verses just cited from First Corinthians 14 to help me facilitate the release of the gifts and ministry through others by controlling the number of times they share or release the gifts in the group or church. I let them know they do have the grace to do this because of the directive from His Word. They can keep silent to allow others to speak and they can control themselves.

Guidelines and Biblical Order

There have been a number of times when I or one of my leaders have requested this person we are addressing to limit the number of times he or she shares to two, and two minutes each in subsequent meetings. I wish I could say each time we have had to confront an individual about this it ended well. Some did and some didn't. The bottom line is, in order to have a move of God and develop a healthy environment for the release of the gifts, leaders must be willing to address individuals who dominate. You also must be willing to lose them if they will not cooperate with the guidelines and biblical order you are establishing.

Paul responds to those who refuse to submit to spiritual authority and biblical order in the release of the gifts in the following way:

> Or did the Word of God come originally from you? Or was it you only that it reached? If anyone thinks himself to be a prophet or spiritual, let him acknowledge that the things which I write to you are the commandments of the Lord. But if anyone is ignorant, let him be ignorant (1 Corinthians 14:36-38).

I believe his response is very clear and requires no explanation from me. I would just add to that, "Selah." Think about it and realize Paul wrote these three chapters in First Corinthians so we would not remain ignorant of spiritual gifts and we could operate them with confidence. Paul's final exhortation to us on the appropriate approach to the gifts are as follows from First Corinthians 14:39-40:

1. Desire earnestly to prophesy.

2. Do not forbid speaking in tongues.

3. Follow my instruction about how the gifts are to be released and function in order.

Chapter 13

CAN WOMEN TEACH AND MINISTER IN THE CHURCH?

What is your experience and what have you been taught regarding women teaching and ministering in the church? So many churches and denominations teach against women ministers, teachers, or pastors. Yet they will allow women to teach in their Sunday school classes, children's ministry, youth ministry, and even on the mission field. Something is wrong with this picture. On one hand they forbid women to minister and teach the adults in a Sunday morning service, but they allow them to teach and minister in almost any other setting in the church. This seems so hypocritical and inequitable to me.

The foundation for this position comes from two passages of Scripture penned by the apostle Paul. One of those passages is located in First Corinthians 14 where Paul is establishing order for the operation of the gifts in the church. I intentionally left that point of order out of the previous chapter in this book. I wanted to spend an entire chapter establishing the truth and setting women and the church free from misunderstanding a woman's role in the church! Let's look together at these two passages:

> *Let your women keep silent in the churches, for they are not permitted to speak; but they are to be submissive, as the law also says. And if they want to learn something, let them ask their own husbands at home; for it is shameful for women to speak in church* (1 Corinthians 14:34-35).

> *Let a woman learn in silence with all submission. And I do not permit a woman to teach or to have authority over a man, but to be in silence. For Adam was formed first, then Eve* (1 Timothy 2:11-13).

These verses that seem to prohibit all women from ministering in the church are *not* directed to *all* women. They are directed to *wives!* How can we be certain of that? Because the only category of women who have husbands are wives. He said, *"let them ask their own husbands at home."* That's not possible for a woman to do if she is not married. Therefore, this passage could not be addressing all women, only wives. The same thing is true for the passage in First Timothy 2. Notice the analogy Paul uses for the woman and man relationship here is Adam and Eve—the first husband and wife.

Relationship Priorities

These passages are not forbidding women from ministering in the church. Rather, they are establishing a principle of order for wives to maintain submission and respect for their husbands while they are using their ministry gifts in the church. Paul is showing us that moving in the gifts and rebelling against or showing disrespect toward your spouse is not compatible. These two passages are specifically forbidding wives to use the church or their ministry as a platform to either expose their husband's ignorance or establish authority over their husband.

These two passages establish a point of order that the marriage relationship is higher priority than the ministry of either spouse. He is revealing to us that operating your ministry or spiritual gifts in the church is not greater than your relationship with your mate. And for the wife, your ministry gifts, responsibilities, and platform in the church do not exempt you from maintaining a submissive heart and attitude toward your husband.

Another way to communicate this is, "Thus saith the Lord" in a prophetic word is never a higher priority than "It is written" and staying with the written Word. Paul is making this principle clear in the two passages in First Corinthians 14 and First Timothy 2. He is essentially saying a wife is not permitted to use her ministry platform to shame her husband, usurp authority over her husband, or attempt to straighten him out. Any wife who attempts to do that is not permitted to speak in the church!

This is not a gender issue but a husband and wife issue he is addressing. Paul was not a woman hater or someone filled with gender prejudice. God would not allow someone who was so disposed to write on His behalf and call it His Word. Neither was Paul addressing this to all women because of the tradition or culture of the day. I have heard some teach he forbade women to speak in church because in that culture the women sat on one side of the church and the men on the other. This created a challenging situation for whenever a wife wanted to speak to her husband she would have to raise her voice and yell to him across the room. Of course this would be very disrupting. Therefore, they assert Paul was really only speaking to the women of that time and culture.

If that were true, then these verses would not apply to us today. And how many other verses or passages in the Bible would be in danger of becoming obsolete because of the same cultural argument? I don't believe that for a moment. Though it may be true the church services in that time looked a lot like what these teachers describe, that does not change the relevancy of the Word of God including these passages regarding women or wives.

Biblical Family Order

Paul was simply establishing a principle of order in the church. That is, the church should always be a place that supports the institution of marriage and proper biblical family order above the individual's ministry in the church. He was also directing church leadership that they must never tolerate a wife's use of her ministry or spiritual gifts in the church to either usurp authority over her husband or publicly embarrass her husband.

The following verse is an example of Jesus' directive along the same lines:

> *Nevertheless I have a few things against you, because you allow that woman Jezebel, who calls herself a prophetess, to teach and seduce My servants to commit sexual immorality and eat things sacrificed to idols* (Revelation 2:20).

Though Queen Jezebel died many years ago, the spirit that controlled her still attempts to infiltrate the church today. If that were not true, why would Jesus be addressing this spirit in the present tense? It is up to spiritual leaders to stop anyone yielding to this type of anti-Christ ministry or behavior. In this verse Jesus is warning church leaders in Thyatira against tolerating her teaching in the church to promote sexual immorality and idolatry. Some other character traits of this type of false ministry is manipulation, witchcraft, and control.

Jezebel was married to King Ahab. Many times this spirit will manifest through married women who have wonderful spiritual gifts but a dysfunctional marriage. I have observed this spirit operating through men as well. Yet every Jezebel needs an Ahab to exist—someone who allows her to promote her selfish, controlling agenda. This is what both Jesus and Paul were addressing and forbidding in the church. The following is another verse that confirms the same principle:

> *But every woman who prays or prophesies with her head uncovered dishonors her head...* (1 Corinthians 11:5).

Again in this passage I believe Paul is primarily addressing wives, not all women. In effect, he is saying, "Wives, stay under your husband's authority while you are praying, prophesying, and using your ministry gifts in the church. Don't allow yourselves to become uncovered and open to the attacks of the enemy by dishonoring your head in your marriage relationship." This next verse amplifies this truth:

> *For this reason the woman ought to have a symbol of authority on her head, because of the angels* (1 Corinthians 11:10).

What does this verse really mean? Let me give you the Greg Mohr translation as the Spirit revealed it to me: "For this reason a wife should remain submitted to and in healthy relationship with her husband because of the angels." What's the issue with the angels? Angels work best with least resistance to accomplish their assignment to bless, protect, and minister to us. This works best where there is love, respect, and the absence of strife in our marriages. Peter confirms this in his epistle when he describes the marriage relationship environment of understanding, honor, and partnering together as essential so your prayers are not hindered (see 1 Peter 3:7).

Ineffective Environment

Allowing an environment of misunderstanding, lack of respect, and strife will actually hinder your prayers by opening the door to the enemy to take advantage of you. This can also limit angels' effectiveness to minister on our behalf according to First Corinthians 11:10. Obviously the responsibility for stewarding our marriage relationship goes both ways—with the husband and the wife. But it is certainly a sobering reality to know the relative health, love, and respect in our marriage relationship can impact the effectiveness of our prayers.

It is also a big deal to God when it comes to the effectiveness and release of our ministry in the church. This is true for both husbands and wives. Paul addresses this in his letter to Timothy regarding husbands and their responsibility for stewarding their marriage and family before their ministry:

> For if a man does not know how to rule his own house, how will he take care of the church of God? (1 Timothy 3:5)

It is clear to me from all the verses we have referenced in this chapter that the Lord has established a higher priority of marriage and family over ministry. That is what Paul is addressing when he brings up the subject of women—wives—speaking and ministering in the church. With this understanding in mind, I want to share with you my paraphrase of First Corinthians 14:34-35: "Wives, if you have questions that are leading or intended to expose your mate or straighten him out, ask it at home, not at the church! Keep silent in the church if that is your motive or hidden agenda."

I have actually experienced this a number of times in some mid-week services in our church where I have allowed a time for questions and answers. In one instance, a woman who was relatively new in our church lifted her hand during the Q&A time. When I recognized her, she made a statement and then asked a question. It went something like this, "Pastor Greg, I have a friend whose husband rarely reads his Bible, will only come to church once a month or so and on special occasions. He also has some bad habits of cussing and smoking. He doesn't listen to his wife, isn't filled with the Spirit or led by the Spirit in his decisions. What should I counsel her to do to help him grow in his relationship with God and listen to his wife?"

In this situation everyone in the church knew the friend she was referencing was actually herself. And the elephant in the room was her husband. It just so happened this was the first mid-week service her husband had attended with her. It was obvious to all and most painfully obvious to her husband she was describing him. Knowing and understanding the principle Paul outlined in First Corinthians 14, I instructed her I would not answer her question that night. I encouraged her to go home and ask her husband what he thought she should counsel her friend.

She was not at all thrilled by my answer. But everyone else who was part of this service took note of that. And it was a long time before any wife risked asking such a question publicly again. Her husband started coming to church more regularly after that. He also began to grow in his relationship with the Lord and his servant leadership role with his wife. Her desire was right but her method was wrong. She was attempting to get my help while her husband was there to straighten him out and shame him into becoming a spiritual leader in her home. That is exactly what Paul is forbidding here in this passage of Scripture.

Colossians 3:19 says, *"Husbands, love your wives and do not be bitter toward them,"* and is in the Bible for a reason. It is a command to husbands to deal with resentment toward their wives for attempting to move them along spiritually or to take the spiritual leadership of their home from them. In other words, being more of a "mama" to them instead of a wife. Wives understand this: your husband doesn't need another mama. He needs a wife who will love him, share her heart with him, pray the Word over him, and then trust the Lord to deal with him and conform him into the image of Christ.

Appropriate Use of Gifts

I have one more paraphrase I want to share with you relating to our understanding that Paul was not speaking to all women in these passages, but to wives. This one comes from First Timothy 2:11-12: "I do not allow the church to be used by a wife to instruct her husband in an attempt to either rebel against him or use the Word to usurp his authority in the home." In our marriage, my wife was filled with the Spirit before me. She had been studying and reading the Word more than me. When I finally was filled with the Spirit, began to seek God and grow in my relationship with the Lord, Janice knew the Bible much better than me. I was intimidated by the amount of verses she could quote and speak in her conversation and in her prayers.

Thankfully she did not use her superior knowledge of the Word against me. If she had, it could have sent me in the other direction spiritually. Yet I have observed this happening in many marriage relationships. One particular couple in our church, James and Betty, were like this. Each of them had known the Lord for a long time when they came to our church. But Betty had come to faith in Christ and was filled with the Spirit ten years before James. So she was well versed in the Bible and taught Bible studies for years before James received the Lord. Betty was a gifted teacher of the Word, but she also made sure James understood she knew the Word better than him.

Whenever he attempted to lead his wife, she would remind him she had been studying the Word much longer than him, was a teacher of the Word, and he didn't really understand what he was reading or was receiving from the Lord as well as she did. Betty was using the functional authority of her teaching gift to attempt to usurp authority over James' delegated authority in their marriage and family. This is exactly what Paul is warning against. Wives are not to use their superior knowledge of the Word or their ministry gift to rebel against their husband's leadership in their lives.

These verses are not forbidding a woman from ministering in the church. Rather they are establishing the appropriate use of the gifts in the church that also upholds proper order, respect, and love in the home. As we complete this chapter, I want to share with you a number of instances in the Word where women ministered in the church.

> *And it shall come to pass in the last days, says God, that I will pour out of My Spirit on all flesh; your sons and daughters shall prophesy...* (Acts 2:17).

Both sons *and* daughters will prophesy *in the church!*

> *On the next day we who were Paul's companions departed and came to Caesarea, and entered the house of Philip the evangelist, who was one of the seven and stayed with him. Now this man had four virgin daughters who prophesied* (Acts 21:8-9).

How did Paul and Luke know Philip's daughters prophesied if they only did that in private? And if they prophesied in some public setting where others heard them, this had to be acceptable, rather than forbidden, for women to speak, teach, or prophesy in church!

> *So he [Apollos] began to speak boldly in the synagogue. When Aquila and Priscilla heard him, they took him aside and explained to him the way of God more accurately* (Acts 18:26).

Obviously Priscilla, Aquila's wife, was a seasoned and gifted teacher of the Word who was used by the Lord alongside her husband to teach Apollos the grace of God.

> *But every woman who prays or prophesies with her head uncovered dishonors her head, for that is one and the same as if her head were shaved* (1 Corinthians 11:5).

This verse speaks of women praying and prophesying in the church.

> *For you can all prophesy...* (1 Corinthians 14:31).

This was written to the entire church, which includes men and women. If all can prophesy in the church, then all would include all women! It is acceptable and needful that women minister, teach, pray, prophesy, and use their gifts in the church. Neither Paul, Jesus, or the Bible prohibits women speaking, teaching, or ministering in the church.

I pray freedom over each woman of God who reads this. Brush the dust off of your gifts. Teach! Preach! Prophesy! Move out in the gifts and calling of God on your life with boldness and confidence. The Lord has need of you. The church has need of you. I speak a release of the anointing of God in and through your life and signs and wonders following the Word you proclaim in Jesus' name!

Chapter 14

HOW TO JUDGE A
PROPHETIC WORD

THERE HAS NEVER BEEN A TIME THE CHURCH HAS NEEDED A GEN-
uine expression of prophetic ministry more than now. This has
always been the case throughout church history. But there is a great
hunger among people seeking God for a real move of the Spirit
and legitimate demonstrations of the Spirit in this hour. This need
must be met by genuine Spirit-filled disciples of Jesus who know the
Word of God and have a personal relationship with the Holy Spirit.

I have known individuals who are so hungry for the supernatural they will accept any substitute that is supernatural, even if it
is a counterfeit. A number of years ago we visited some long-time
friends of ours, Mike and Tracy, in another state while on vacation.
They graciously invited us to spend the night with them instead of

incurring the expense of a hotel. We gladly accepted and enjoyed catching up with them over a wonderful dinner.

After dinner, Janice and Tracy were cleaning up the kitchen while Mike and I enjoyed some coffee in the living room. Knowing I was a pastor, he brought up a nightly show he had been enjoying on late night TV he described as very spiritual. Mike was a believer but was attending a denominational church that did not emphasize the teaching of the Word or the authority of the Word in the life of the believer. He began to describe to me how the host of this TV show would walk through the audience and tell individuals messages he was receiving from their loved ones who had passed away.

I listened in shock as he described how accurate this man was in his description of their passed loved ones. This TV "prophet" would share in great detail things about their life on earth, their occupation, hobbies, desires, etc. prior to their death. Then he would typically tell them something their loved one wanted to share with their living family member. I wasn't in shock because of the things this false prophet did but that my good friend Mike believed this was from God. I told him, "Mike, this guy is operating by a familiar spirit, not the Holy Spirit!"

He replied, "Yea, I know. That spirit is telling those people everything about their loved one's lives who had passed away. This has to be God." I tried for close to an hour to persuade Mike this guy was a false prophet that was evil and not good. But he would not be swayed from his belief this was good and was God. I was not able to get through to him because of his hunger for the supernatural and his ignorance of the Word of God. The Bible calls these kinds of "supernatural" demonstrations as coming from an angel of light.

*For such are false apostles, deceitful workers, transforming themselves into apostles of Christ. And no wonder! For **satan himself transforms himself into an angel of light**. Therefore it is no great thing if his ministers also transform themselves into ministers of righteousness, whose end will be according to their works* (2 Corinthians 11:13-15).

We must take the time to know and understand the Word of God or we can be subject to deception by counterfeit ministers and counterfeit demonstrations. This is why I have such a passion for genuine prophetic ministry. I have observed and known of several "non-profit" prophets over the past four decades of involvement in Spirit-filled churches and ministry. Some of these gave out "words" for an offering. Others only gave "tragedy and death, gloom and doom" words. Others I have observed had a "word" every day for every person in every situation. A few others I observed were real false prophets who were wolves in sheep's clothing. Their only agenda was to come in to the church, devour immature sheep with their lies and deception, and connect them to their cult-like group.

I have also seen and known some true prophets and true prophetic ministries that brought great blessing to the church and individuals. Because of the propensity of the prophetic to bless people as well as hurt them when the wrong people are using this precious gift, it is essential we train people how to properly judge prophecy and prophetic words. The Word of God certainly bears this out:

Do not despise prophecies. Test all things; hold fast what is good (1 Thessalonians 5:20-21).

Let two or three prophets speak, and let the others judge (1 Corinthians 14:29).

All prophecies, prophetic words, and declarations must be tested and judged. How can we test and judge these things and know which ones to believe and hold fast to and which ones to reject? Over the years I have received hundreds of prophetic words. Many of them were from God. Others weren't even close to being from the Lord. I want to share with you the key principles I use to judge and test prophetic words.

1. *Does the word you received line up with the written Word?*

> *And since we have the same spirit of faith, according to what is written, "I believed and therefore I spoke," we also believe and therefore speak* (2 Corinthians 4:13).

The Lord is not going to give you a word that violates His written Word. The reason why many people have difficulty hearing the Lord accurately is they place prophecies, dreams, visions, and other supernatural ways God can speak to us above the written Word. That is a recipe for deception, disaster, and great disappointment in your life. In order to hear the Lord clearly and judge a prophetic word accurately, it requires us to *value the written Word above all other supernatural means God can speak to us.* You must determine that no prophetic word ever has higher authority in your heart and mind than God's written Word.

> *For He received from God the Father honor and glory, when there came such a voice to him from the Excellent Glory: "This My beloved Son, in whom I am well pleased." And we heard this voice which came from heaven when we were with Him on the holy mountain. And so we have the **prophetic word confirmed**, which you do well to heed, as a light that shines in a dark place,*

until the day dawns and the morning star rises in your hearts (2 Peter 1:17-19).

This is an amazing passage of Scripture. Peter declares he heard the audible voice of God from Heaven speak over Jesus. Then he tells us we have the prophetic word confirmed—a more sure word of prophecy—than the audible voice of God. That is the written Word of God! The first thing I do when someone gives me a prophetic word is I take time to check it out by making certain it lines up with the written Word. You and I are never obligated to act on a prophetic word—no matter who gives it to you—until you check it out by the written Word.

2. Does it witness to your spirit?

Is the prophecy something your heart bears witness with? Does it confirm what God has already been dealing with you about? Is it peaceful or confusing?

> *The Spirit Himself bears witness with our spirit that we are children of God* (Romans 8:16).

If He will bear witness with our spirit we are His children, He will also bear witness of other things He is leading us to do as His children. The second thing I do when receiving a prophetic word to test and judge it is to check out how it witnesses with my spirit and the Holy Spirit in me. If it doesn't immediately witness with me I set that word on the shelf. And I will only visit that again if the Spirit leads me to consider it.

3. Does it pass the test of counsel from spiritual leaders in your life?

> *Let two or three prophets speak, and let the others judge* (1 Corinthians 14:29).

The Word instructs us to have prophetic words judged by other mature leaders and/or prophets in the church. Why is that necessary if the individual giving the word is certain the Lord has spoken to him or her? Because any of us can miss it when we run what we think the Lord is speaking to us through the screen of our brain. Our individual perspective can be skewed. Our heart could be hurt and we do not realize it. Or our limited knowledge of the Word can affect how we translate what the Lord is speaking to us.

Each of us has blind spots and experiences that can cause us to misapply or wrongly interpret what God is speaking to us. Most of the time we are not missing the fact God is speaking to us. The problem lies in the translation of what we believe He is saying. This makes it imperative we have other mature leaders and disciples of Jesus judge the prophetic word someone gives to us.

Several years ago in a time of prayer and seeking the Lord, I believe I heard Him speak to me saying that He had a new assignment for my wife and me. It was a very strong impression in my heart that startled me because we had a very successful church and ministry at the time. I didn't say anything to Janice about this immediately and just spent a bit more time praying over it.

Within an hour of the time God spoke to me, a good friend of mine and a prophet to our church, Ron Smith, called me. He said, "Pastor Greg, I have just come from a time of prayer and the Lord told me to call you and tell you to get ready, He has a new assignment for you and Janice!"

Wow! What a powerful confirmation of what the Lord had spoken to me just an hour before. After Ron's call to me, I let Janice know what I believed I had heard from God and the prophetic word Ron spoke to me. She agreed and confirmed what the Lord and Ron Smith revealed to me. Two days later we met with our pastor, Bob Nichols, to ask him to judge this word. I also shared it with a couple of other trusted ministry friends to ask for their counsel on this. Each of these men confirmed to us they felt we had heard from God. They also counseled us to walk it out with patience and not attempt to self-fulfill this word. That was great counsel.

The reality is, Janice and I are now living in the fulfillment of that word that God had a new assignment for us. Godly counsel confirmed this word and helped us to walk out the Lord's timing on it. No matter how supernatural the direction we believe we received from the Lord, it is still important to have trusted leaders and friends help us judge its validity. It is also helpful to receive counsel on how to step into the new direction with faith and wisdom. In this case, the counsel we received was crucial in helping us walk into the new assignment the Lord had for us.

> *Without counsel, plans go awry, but in the multitude of counselors they are established* (Proverbs 15:22).

One final note on this point: when receiving counsel from others, I rarely allow the counsel to sway me off what I am sensing God has spoken. However, many times the counsel helps me to discern more accurately the strategy and timing of the fulfillment of that word.

4. A true prophetic word will lead you toward God and build you up.

True prophecy will not lead you to compromise with evil or sin. With some prophetic words there is no absolute way to judge whether it is of God or not. The reason for this is the subjective nature of some prophecies. For example, if someone receives a word they should go into business, move to a different city, or change jobs. There is nothing in the Word either endorsing or forbidding those things.

In these cases, you simply have to give things time to determine the fruit of that word. Did it work out for the individual? Did it cause them to draw closer to the Lord and His purpose for their lives? Or did pursuing that word cause there to be a spiritual decline in their life?

> He who prophesies speaks edification and exhortation
> and comfort to men (1 Corinthians 14:3).

Exhortation means to draw near to God. As spiritual leaders we need to watch for the fruit in the lives of those who receive a prophetic word. Does that word cause them to draw near to the Lord, live more Christlike, and have a positive, God-centered influence on their family, friends, and acquaintances or something else? Does it leave them with faith and hope or discouragement and despair? A true prophetic word will lead you toward God and build you up.

5. Realize that divine timing is involved with divine promise.

Some words are "now" words and some are "future" words. We all love those "now" words, but we have to pray over and discern the timing of each prophetic word we receive.

> Searching what, or what manner of time, the Spirit
> of Christ who was in them was indicating... (1 Peter
> 1:11).

It is not only important for us to recognize what the Lord is saying but also the timing or season for its fulfillment.

> ...to every purpose there is time and judgment...
> (Ecclesiastes 8:6 KJV).

This is a very practical and revealing verse on discerning God's timing. The purpose is the "what" you received as a download from the Lord to do, whether through a prophetic word or inward witness. Time is the when. The judgment is the strategy or the how. My experience in discerning His timing has taught me the timing of the word is closely related to the revelation of the how or the strategy to fulfill it.

I was praying for a new worship leader for our church several years ago because ours was no longer able to make the commitment needed to lead the team. During that time, I went to a conference and attended a prayer service one morning. The prophet leading the service called me out and said he had a word for me. He said the Lord told him to tell me, "Concerning the thing you have been praying about, all you need is already in your house."

Wow! That was certainly a "now" word that revealed to me my new worship leader was already in our church. After praying over this, the Lord confirmed to me our new worship leader was our drummer. So we brought him out from behind the drums, he began to lead worship and became our worship leader for more than ten years. Praise God for true prophetic words that are "now" words.

There was another time a minister I knew came up to me during a prayer and worship service and told me he saw me pastoring two churches. I had to pray over that word because the church I was pastoring at the time was going through a very challenging season. Though this word did resonate in my heart, I felt it was a "future" word I was to simply pray over and God would show me the right time it would be fulfilled. It was fulfilled two years later when the Lord showed me the city twenty-five miles north of the town we lived is where we were to plant the new church.

I love "now" words, but don't make the mistake of trying to make a "future" word a "now" word. You have the ability to discern not only what God is telling you to do but also "what manner of time" it is to be fulfilled!

6. *Most prophecies are conditional.*

True prophecies are a divine invitation into your kingdom potential. But they are not automatic. They require human cooperation. God does His part when we do our part—repentance, obedience, trust, etc. God spoke to Elijah to go hide by the Brook Cherith during a time of famine (1 Kings 17:2-4). He said He had commanded the ravens to feed him there. In order for Elijah to receive the provision this word promised him, he had to go to the specific brook the Lord spoke to him about. Had he either stayed where he was or gone to any other brook, this word would not have been fulfilled.

Once we have tested, judged, and proven a prophetic word is valid and from the Lord, we must provide corresponding action— our obedience that comes from faith. The word the Lord gave me about pastoring two churches was both a strong and challenging word. I had to come into agreement with it and then take action once I knew the time was right. The action steps we took stretched us and cost a lot of money. But the outcome was worth the investment. However, had we not added corresponding actions to the word the Lord gave us, we would not have seen this great new church built and all the lives transformed who attended there.

7. *A prophetic word never stands alone.*

> *For we know in part and prophesy in part* (1 Corinthians 13:9).

This is a very important principle to learn in regard to prophecy. No prophetic word is ever the entire message. Notice it says, *"we prophesy in part."* Some prophets or individuals who give a prophetic word act as though that word is the beginning to the end of all we ever need to hear from God. It is not. It is part. It may be a very important part of what God is telling us, but it is never the whole.

Most prophecies are focused on the destination or goal rather than the journey or process. It's a lot like some of the ads we see for destination vacations. They tell you all about the glorious things you will experience when you get there—the ocean breeze and views, the wonderful food, rest and relaxation, etc.—but they say nothing about how much work it took to save the money to go and all the packing to get ready. They also don't tell you about the delays at the airport or the timeshare agents who will hound you at the hotel when you arrive. Nor do they tell you the two tall weeds outside of your window that's supposed to be a "garden view." Neither do they tell you about the air conditioner that doesn't work in your room or the slippery tile floor on which your wife will fall and get hurt.

This is actually what happened to us a few years ago on an all-inclusive vacation. It actually ended up very good as they gave us a new room with an ocean view. My point is, when the Lord gives you a word, it is more about the destination and less about the process to get there. We cannot depend on additional prophetic words to help us on our journey. We have to walk that out by faith.

> *By the mouth of two or three witnesses every word will be established* (2 Corinthians 13:1).

A prophetic word never stands alone. It must have the support of the written Word, the inward witness of our spirit, and godly counsel. We are not responsible to act on any prophetic word alone. But once we have tested the word and proven it valid, we still have to take steps of faith each day in walking it out and fulfilling it.

8. Hold fast to the prophetic words you have proven to be true.

> *Do not despise prophecies. Test all things; hold fast what is good* (1 Thessalonians 5:20-21).

> *This charge I commit to you, son Timothy, according to the prophecies previously made concerning you, that by them you may wage the good warfare* (1 Timothy 1:18).

I encourage you to write down the prophecies that have been spoken over you so you can meditate on them and consider the kingdom potential God sees in you. Whenever someone gives me a prophecy, I ask them to write it down or email it to me. After I have proven it to be from the Lord, I put it into a file called "Prophetic Words." Then I go back from time to time and meditate on those words. I consider what the Lord is saying about my kingdom potential and how it will be when I am walking in the fullness of that word.

I meditate on it until I see myself in it. That becomes my new reality rather than what I see in the natural realm. Then I begin to speak it out, especially when the enemy sends opposition against that word. That's what Paul meant by waging the good warfare with these prophecies. The good warfare is one you win. Since Jesus has already won the war, you and I will experience the victory and success His Word and prophetic words promise if we embrace them, see ourselves in them, and speak them out.

You are more than a conqueror through Christ and His Word to you!

Chapter 15

RECEIVING A PROPHET

I BELIEVE THE PROPHET'S MINISTRY IS ONE OF THE MOST MISUN-derstood of any of the five-fold ministry offices Jesus gave to the church. One of the reasons for this is the modern-day church does not have as widespread exposure to this ministry gift as it does some of the others. Most of the church is very familiar with the pastor, teacher, and evangelist because these are the three that have had the most exposure.

Yet we do see several examples of the ministry of the prophet in the Word, especially the Old Testament. Some of these prophets were Moses, Samuel, Elijah, Elisha, Nathan, Gad, Jeremiah, Isaiah, Joel, John the Baptist, Jesus, Paul, and Agabus. In the Old Testament, the prophet's ministry was more about communicating to the people what God was saying because the people did not have the Holy Spirit dwelling in them.

In the New Testament—the church age we are in—the prophet's ministry is more about alerting us to what the Lord has already spoken and we have not yet aligned ourselves with it. Or it is about focusing us on something the Lord is preparing for us in the future that we can draw on our relationship with the Lord to walk out.

As mentioned previously, a prophet came to our church at least once a year for the twenty-four years I pastored in Decatur, Texas. His name was Ron Smith. Ron was also an excellent teacher of the Word. But when he came to our church, I asked him to step into the prophet's office and anointing because our church already was exposed to the teacher ministry office. I wanted the congregation to learn to receive from another dimension of the five-fold ministry offices, the prophet's ministry.

I would normally schedule him for three to five days of ministry in the summer time when people did not have school schedules to be concerned with. Each time he came I would take time to prepare the people for Brother Ron's prophetic ministry. There were always new people I needed to prepare so they would know how to receive him. I would let them know that Prophet Ron Smith was coming to town for a several-day meeting. I encouraged them to be open and expect the gifts of the Spirit to manifest in these services. I encouraged them not to turn him off if he did something a bit unusual. Prophets are known for that.

I let them know he most likely would not be teaching line by line in his ministry of the Word. Instead, he would be dropping Holy Spirit "smart bombs" to destroy the enemy's plans against them and to blast people out of unbelief. I let them know he would be operating strongly in words of knowledge, words of wisdom, discerning of spirits, gifts of healing, and working of miracles. Once I prepared them, there was a great expectancy in the church. And it never failed; we saw some amazing supernatural things in those meetings.

People were healed, received direction, correction, instruction, restoration of marriage relationships, calling from God, and on and on. We always experienced a powerful move of the Spirit when Prophet Ron Smith came to our church. And the impartation of his ministry began to become part of the DNA of our church.

> *He who receives a prophet in the name of a prophet shall receive a prophet's reward* (Matthew 10:41).

The Bible teaches us there is a specific reward for receiving the prophet's ministry appropriately. Essentially this means we are open to the prophet and celebrate his ministry rather than just tolerate it. The reason some just tolerate the prophet's ministry is because of some of the unique character traits of this ministry. Each prophet is unique, but almost always each has some quirks and idiosyncrasies that can cause people to close their hearts off to him or her.

Brother Ron Smith was from Oklahoma and was one quarter Indian heritage. Many times he was with us he would do an Indian dance as he was prompted by the Spirit. He used this dance to take authority over the enemy as he described "dancing on the enemy's head because he is under our feet." This would put some religious people off, but there was always something very powerful that would occur in bringing freedom to others who received it.

We are called to receive this ministry—celebrate it, not tolerate it! What our church experienced over those twenty-four years of receiving the prophet's ministry was nothing short of supernatural. We saw people saved and healed each year. Words of knowledge and words of wisdom gave strength and courage to individuals. When the prophet came to town, our counseling demand from church members was nonexistent. The reason for this is when the gifts are in operation and the prophet is speaking directly to people's hearts and dealing with root issues in their lives, they begin to seek God and hear from Him on their own.

The benefits to our church and individual members from the prophet's ministry were numerous. And they were both spiritual and natural. There is a reward for giving the welcome due a prophet—because of the office he functions in as sent by God. One example of this can be found in Second Kings chapter 4. This is the story of the barren woman who built the prophet Elisha a prophet's quarters so he could have a place to stay when he was in the area. She was rewarded with a son and subsequently, her son was raised from the dead later. That is quite a powerful reward for simply receiving the prophet and celebrating his ministry.

Powerful Visitation

I want to tell you about a very powerful visitation I received regarding the prophet's ministry several years ago. I dropped off two of my children at a children's summer camp for a week in Kerrville, Texas. As I was driving back to North Texas, I passed by the Lyndon Johnson ranch. I pulled over to the side of the road to view this vast ranch of one of our former presidents. While I was looking out the driver's side window I sensed someone or something got into my car. I looked back to the right at the passenger side of the car and my car was filled with a very bright fog, almost like smoke or haze.

Then I heard a voice come out of that haze saying, "Jesus the Prophet has come to your body but you did not recognize Him. He has come and will come again if you will receive Him. The prophet mantle has come to your body and you have not recognized it. Do not miss your day of visitation. He will come again if you desire that gift, receive Him and don't settle for the familiar."

I was trembling at this presence in my car. I wasn't sure at first if it was the Holy Spirit or an angel. I really believe this was an angel because later as I was praying in the Spirit, the Holy Spirit began to download to me the revelation of what the prophet's ministry looks like. It was like the Spirit began to unpack for me what the angel had just spoken to me. I knew exactly what he meant when he said "Jesus the Prophet has come to your body but you did not recognize Him."

When he said this, it was like film clips of specific services were re-run in my mind. Each were times when the presence of God was so electric and the revelation of the Word was so powerful, but we just passed them off as normal or familiar. Sometimes it came through Ron Smith the prophet. Other times it came through me or Paul Milligan, a teaching elder in my church.

What I understood through this visitation was when Jesus the Prophet was ministering in our church, the anointing on that ministry was different. In these times He was bringing revelation on a particular truth He wanted us to take time to unpack and teach over a period of time. Or there was something else He wanted us to focus on in a particular ministry or outreach. And He had manifested Himself many more times than we were aware. It wasn't just through the prophet, Ron Smith that Jesus the Prophet manifested Himself. He had come at other times and through other ministers, but because none of those were known to function in the office of the prophet, we did not regard these the same.

As I began to pray in the Spirit and meditate on this visitation, the haze lifted out of my car. I was too shaken to drive right away. I began to ask the Holy Spirit to show me how to recognize Jesus the Prophet when He visited our church again. I also wanted to know how He wanted to bring genuine prophetic ministry to the church and through whom.

I found my briefcase, took out a pen and paper and began to write down the things the Spirit revealed to me about the prophet's ministry. The following are the traits of the prophet the Spirit made real to me that day. The prophet's ministry:

1. Brings light on the specific part of God's promise or your destiny He is focused on fulfilling at this time.

2. Gives light on our future inheritance that brings us hope.

3. Expands us spiritually—gives us eyes to see and ears to hear.

4. Expands our vision to see the big picture—the gestalt.

5. Reveals what part of the Word He is emphasizing at this time, the heart strategies and plans of God.

6. Arrests satan's attempts to stop God's promise to us by:
   a. Revelation—discerning of spirits, words of knowledge and words of wisdom that reveal what is going on in the spirit realm so we are not deceived.
   b. Miracles—that change the course of satan's plans against us. Example: Holy Spirit smart bombs.

7. Adds new dimension to present knowledge.
   a. Acts 7:17: *"But when the time of the promise drew near which God had sworn to Abraham, the people grew and multiplied in Egypt."*

8. Helps us stay current with what God is saying and doing at this point in time.

a. Luke 4:21: *"Today this Scripture is fulfilled in your hearing."*

9. There is a different anointing on the Word when Jesus the Prophet comes. It is not better necessarily but usually contains a very strong presence of God and the message is clear, simple, and direct that grabs the attention of the people.

10. Prophets do have a ministry of the Word, but not usually line upon line.

I spent about an hour on the side of the road that afternoon writing down these things the Holy Spirit downloaded to me about the prophet's ministry. What I saw was Jesus the Prophet had actually been attempting to reveal Himself in that facet of ministry but we had failed to recognize Him and value Him doing that through anyone else other than the prophet Ron Smith. I saw that He would visit us in this capacity from time to time even through those who did not officially operate in the office of the prophet.

I think I learned more about the prophet's ministry that day than all of the messages I had heard about this office in the past. The prophet will stir up the supernatural in the church. He will also release a flow of the gifts through the body by his or her obedience to manifest the gifts.

Prophets lay the axe to the root. Pastors and teachers have to follow up and clean up. Prophets speak pointedly about the specific direction the Lord wants the church to focus on. Pastors and teachers follow up and provide the principles and tools from the Word to fulfill that direction.

> *...Believe in the Lord your God, and you shall be established; believe His prophets, and you shall prosper* (2 Chronicles 20:20).

There is value and reward to recognizing and receiving the prophet's ministry.

Chapter 16

PRACTICAL GUIDELINES FOR OPERATING THE GIFTS

The things I am going to share in this chapter apply primarily to pastors and spiritual leaders who want to facilitate and lead people to operate in the gifts in a public service at church or a small group. Yet, these are certainly things we can all learn and benefit from because you may be called on to lead in the future. Knowing these things will help you become better equipped to facilitate the supernatural and the move of the Spirit through God's people.

There are some questions you must ask and answers you must resolve in determining how the gifts will operate under your leadership. The first question is *when* will you allow these gifts to function in a service you are leading? Anytime someone has a word to share?

Or only in one or two places in a service? For example, only after a worship time or only at the end of a service after the ministry of the Word is finished? In any service or just services that have its singular focus on worship and releasing the gifts?

The second question is *who* will you allow to operate in the gifts publicly? Anyone present the Lord is prompting? Only those you know well? Or only staff and leadership?

Another question is *how* will you allow the gifts to operate or function in order under your leadership? At the will of the individual? Only when you recognize an individual after lifting their hand? Requiring individuals who feel they have a word to submit that first to a designated leader in the service? Only at your direction or the lead person directing the service?

Another key question is *how* will you judge the gifts? Publicly? Privately? Not at all? Also, *how* will you explain the scriptural basis for the operation of the gifts when unbelievers or uninformed believers are present? When it occurs? Later at a more convenient time? Not at all?

Another question is *what* gifts or demonstrations of the Spirit will you allow? Tongues? Prophecy? Dance? Choreographed dance? Flags and banners?

Another important question to ask regarding the operation of the gifts is *why* are you going to allow the gifts to operate in the church or small group? To accommodate the more prophetically inclined folks? To bless and edify the body? To release people to function in ministry? Because it pleases the Father when you lead people to experience and move out in the release of the gifts?

One final question to ask is if you decide not to release the operation of the gifts in your church service or small group, *why?* Is it because of conviction? Fear of people? Or an attempt to protect the body from a few who use the gifts to either draw attention to themselves or in a way that makes everyone uncomfortable?

To Dance or Not to Dance

Several years ago, there was a lady in our church who was a professional dancer, had trained in dance for years, and had a business and ministry to train other young girls and women in choreographed dance. They would play worship songs as the background to their choreographed dances and it was really something beautiful to see. She trained the girls to use their dance as personal worship to the Lord. The dances I had seen were quite powerful and anointed, bringing the presence of God each time I had observed them.

Most of these dances had been scheduled at other venues or one or two mid-week services at our church. She asked permission to schedule a dance for our Sunday morning service and we put that on our church calendar. It was to take about seven minutes of our worship service. There were three girls in her team who danced that morning. Two of them were in their late teens and one was in her early twenties. The worship song they selected was great. But there was a major problem with what these young girls were wearing that morning. Each of them had on white, tight, tight, white, tight, *tight, white* yoga pants and spandex tops. I think you can understand my explanation here. There was nothing left to the imagination.

I know these girls were worshiping the Lord with their dance but my North Texas "bubbas," which included most of the men in my church, were not worshiping God during that painfully long seven-minute dance. What was intended to be a blessing and a real worship experience turned out to be a disaster because of their attire.

I had to meet with this choreograph dance instructor and instruct her on the ways of modesty and appropriate dress more perfectly. We didn't cut out the choreographed dancing altogether in our church after that, but we did establish guidelines for the appropriate demonstration of dance performances in the future.

Guidelines for Liberty and Order

In the same way, we established guidelines in our church for the purpose of establishing a healthy balance between liberty and order in the release of the gifts and various demonstrations of the Spirit. First of all, I taught these guidelines in a month-long series on Sunday mornings. Then I also gave the same instruction to all new members in our church. It was included in the new member packet, distributed to all our life group leaders, and available to anyone who had any questions about what we believed and allowed in the release of the gifts in our church. The following is a list of those guidelines:

1. Exalt Jesus—not yourself.
    a. Drawing attention to yourself with various demonstrations and manifestations of the gifts is not appropriate.

2. Make sure the prophetic word you share lines up with the written Word.

3. Every prophecy or public manifestation or demonstration of the gifts will be judged in light of the Word by church leadership, in accordance with First Corinthians 14:29 and First Thessalonians 5:21.

4. Do not share a prophetic utterance publicly unless you can receive correction without taking it as personal rejection.
    a. In the event correction becomes necessary, someone in leadership will get with you in private and not correct you in public.

5. Make love and edifying others your primary goal in operating in spiritual gifts (1 Corinthians 14:1,12).

6. No public correction of individuals through prophecy is allowed.

7. We ask if you have a personal word for someone in the body you take a mature member or leader in the church with you for the purpose of judging that word in light of the Word (1 Corinthians 14:29; 1 Thessalonians 5:21).

8. Personal words to guests and new people must be submitted first to someone in leadership—staff, elders, pastor.

9. Do not speak out publicly in a message in tongues without using your faith to interpret—either you or someone else (1 Corinthians 14:13-19,28).

10. Don't dominate the floor.
    a. Stand up, speak up, and shut up.
    b. *"But if anything is revealed to another who sits by, let the first keep silent"* (1 Corinthians 14:30).
    c. When releasing one of the vocal gifts, do not give a testimony or attempt to teach.

11. Submit what you have to leadership and trust them with the timing and appropriateness of the release of that gift.
    a. Either lift your hand to be recognized by the person leading the service or submit what you have to the assigned gatekeeper at the front of the church.

b. Once you have submitted your word or leading from the Lord in one of these two ways, the responsibility is now on leadership to determine if it is released. Trust the Lord and your leaders with this now. It is no longer your responsibility to bring this forward.

12. Don't be afraid to make mistakes.

a. You will make mistakes, but that will not stop the move of the Spirit or grieve the Holy Spirit.

b. What grieves Him more is when you hold back what He is trying to say or do through you.

When we established these guidelines for our members regarding the release of the gifts in our church services and life groups, it produced really good fruit and results. It caused great peace among the people, biblical order in the operation of the gifts, and it actually encouraged more people to be involved in releasing the gifts.

I also established a set of guidelines for the leaders of our life groups and other leaders in our church who helped me direct the services from time to time. This set of guidelines had more to do with how to facilitate the move of the Spirit and release of the gifts in an orderly way.

Gatekeepers

In our Sunday morning services, we established "gatekeepers" who were various leaders in the church who were responsible to sit in the front of the church on their assigned service day. It was their responsibility to help me judge words or leadings of the Lord submitted by members of the congregation. The people had been instructed who the gatekeepers were. They knew if they had something for the congregation they felt was from the Lord they needed to either bring that in a written message or a verbal communication to one of the gatekeepers.

The gatekeepers would then bring me the words or messages they felt were appropriate for the congregation and that service. I would then typically recognize and release that individual to share what they had received from the Lord. This worked very well for us. We have actually instituted gatekeepers at Charis Bible College worship services now to establish order and regulate the words the students want to share with the student body. We had to do that after a first-year student got up and said publicly, "The Holy Spirit is blue today." I don't know what he meant by that, but it certainly created some confusion among the student body.

Our gatekeepers are a great help to us screening out words that are not appropriate, unbiblical, or not for the entire congregation. This is also a great leadership training ground for developing leaders who desire to facilitate the release of the gifts and the move of the Spirit in the church today. I wanted to give you this background of our reasoning for establishing gatekeepers. This is one of the guidelines I established in my church for our leaders in facilitating the release of the gifts.

The following is the list of guidelines we established for our leaders regarding the release of the gifts:

1. Connect with the assigned gatekeepers prior to the service for any instruction or encouragement.

2. Allow only those you know to share a word, whether they lift their hand or submit a word to one of the gatekeepers.
    a. Know those who labor among you (see 1 Thessalonians 5:12 KJV).

b. Those you do not know, you cannot be certain whether they have a personal agenda, false doctrine, or something else they want to promote through their use of the gifts.

c. If someone you don't know shares a word with one of the gatekeepers and you feel it is a good word for the body, it is acceptable to allow them to give that word.

d. If someone you don't know lifts their hand to be recognized to share a word, ask them to please hold that word and submit it to one of the gatekeepers. Only if the Spirit speaks to you to have them share are you to release someone new or someone you do not know to share.

3. When a word is given publicly, ask the Holy Spirit to show you how we are to respond to that word.

a. Sometimes it is appropriate to ask the person who gave the word to pray that out and lead the congregation to agree about that. Other times it may be appropriate for you to lead the congregation in prayer over that word.

b. Other times there are specific points of action we are to do to respond to it, such as specific prayer, praise, giving, taking authority over the enemy, etc.

4. With each public word, gift, or demonstration of the Spirit, take time to explain to the congregation what they just experienced and give them the biblical reference for that gift or manifestation.

5. When someone on the worship team sings out in tongues through their microphone, require them to follow up with singing in English or the interpretation of what they sang in tongues, even if it is simply praise.

   a. *"What is the conclusion then? I will pray with the spirit, and I will also pray with the understanding. I will sing with the spirit, and I will also sing with the understanding"* (1 Corinthians 14:15).

   b. We do this to eliminate confusion with the expression of the gifts and to align ourselves with the Word.

6. Don't allow more than three prophecies and/or messages in tongues and interpretation of tongues at any one time in the service.

   a. Ask anyone who lifts their hand or wants to share after that to hold what they have because we have already received the limit of words for this time according to the Scripture (1 Corinthians 14:27,29).

7. Make sure any public message in tongues is interpreted (1 Corinthians 14:27).

   a. If no one in the congregation interprets the message within thirty to sixty seconds, either use your faith to give the interpretation or ask the person who gave the message in tongues to interpret it (1 Corinthians 14:15).

Establishing this set of guidelines for our church members and the set of guidelines for our church leaders produced tremendous results in our church. It brought peace to our body. Our people felt safe as there was a pathway of order for the gifts to operate in line with the Word. It caused more people to feel liberty to step out in releasing the gifts with confidence. And it helped raise up leaders who could lead the release of the gifts without quenching the Spirit. The fruit of this was a greater release of the gifts and people who knew how to flow in the supernatural!

Whether you implement any part of these guidelines we used or not, I would encourage every pastor and spiritual leader to seek the Holy Spirit about how you can equip your people and leaders to operate the gifts in biblical order. I pray increase over you, your ministry and church in the flow of the supernatural and the release of the gifts of the Spirit in Jesus' name.

Chapter 17

CREATING AN ENVIRONMENT WHERE THE GIFTS WORK BEST

THERE ARE SOME ESSENTIAL PREPARATION KEYS FOR MAKING THE local church, small groups, and ministries a place where the Holy Spirit has the freedom for His gifts to function through His people. There are some common denominators I have discovered that either hinder or release the flow of the supernatural in the body today.

As I shared in the first chapter of this book, I did not experience the operation of the gifts or the flow of the supernatural in any of the churches I attended for the first twenty-three years of my life. There were some common traits that characterized each of these churches and limited what God was able to do there.

> *How often they provoked Him in the wilderness, and grieved Him in the desert! Yes, again and again they tempted God, and limited the Holy One of Israel* (Psalm 78:40-41).

According to this passage of Scripture, it is possible we can limit God. God is not our problem. He is not holding out on us. He has provided us the fullness of the Spirit, all of these nine wonderful gifts of the Spirit, and the ability to operate in this today. Because Jesus did it, we can do it. Because the early church did it, we can do it. We have the same Spirit, the same Word, the same name, the same power, and the same gifts as they had. Even though this is true, not everyone in the church receives or operates in these gifts.

Many times it is simply churches and church leaders who are limiting God. Many of them are very sincere, but sincerely wrong. They invite the Holy Spirit to come when He is already there and waiting on the leader or leaders to yield to Him. They pray prayers saying the Holy Spirit can have His way in their services but they create service plans and lead the service like He isn't anywhere in sight. The Holy Spirit is not going to force His gifts or the supernatural on us.

> **LEADERS WHO ARE FEARFUL AND IGNORANT OF THE GIFTS AND THE PERSON OF THE HOLY SPIRIT UNKNOWINGLY LIMIT WHAT GOD CAN DO.**

I also have observed a number of churches and church leaders who embrace the Holy Spirit, the gifts of the Spirit, and the supernatural. Their services are dynamic and there is a spirit of expectancy among the people. Through both of these examples—churches and church leaders who limit the move of the Spirit and those who are yielding to the Holy Spirit and experiencing the supernatural in their services and ministry—the Lord has taught me some keys to creating an environment where the gifts and the supernatural work best. That is the purpose of this chapter.

The following five principles are essential in having a church or ministry where the Holy Spirit is not limited and is free to release His gifts through His people.

Pray the Word over the people.

Pray the people would pursue love and desire spiritual gifts (1 Corinthians 14:1). Pray the Lord gives them utterance and they may speak boldly as they ought (Ephesians 6:19). Pray over them that they come behind in no good gift (1 Corinthians 1:7). Pray for a yielding to the Spirit in the leaders and people. Pray for a revelation of love and courage to overcome timidity in moving out in the gifts (Ephesians 3:17-19; 2 Timothy 1:7). Pray the entire church be filled with the Spirit and walk in relationship with and be led by the Spirit (Acts 2:4,38-39; Romans 8:14).

Stand against deception, lies, and wrong teaching in the past by taking authority over the enemy in the lives of your people. Pray for a revelation of the truth for each of them (Ephesians 1:17-20). We are not begging the Holy Spirit to do what He already wants to do. We are just giving Him permission to be both resident and President in the church.

Teach the Word on the gifts.

Teach in small groups, with your leaders and larger corporate gatherings. Anytime the Word is taught it produces faith in the people to act on what is taught.

*So then faith comes by hearing, and hearing by the word
of God* (Romans 10:17).

Prayer is not enough to see a move of the Spirit and release
of the gifts in your church, ministry, small group, or in your life.
Prayer does assist in opening people's hearts to receive the Word
and break off lies and deception in people's minds. People still need
to be taught the Word. There is no substitute for planting the seed
of the Word into people's hearts. It was not possible for me to have
faith to see the supernatural in my life in those churches that never
taught on that subject. It is essential to find a church that teaches
the Word in this area.

This gives the Holy Spirit something to work with. He confirms the Word with signs following (Mark 16:20). This book,
Flowing in the Supernatural, is full of principles and examples from
the Word you could teach in your small group, Bible study class, or
church. If you teach on it, people will receive it, believe it, embrace
it, and act on it. Not everyone will respond in faith immediately. But
don't allow yourself to get discouraged by that. Keep preaching and
teaching the Word on these things and signs will absolutely follow.

*Here am I and the children whom the Lord has given me!
We are for signs and for wonders…* (Isaiah 8:18).

Signs are to follow the believers. Believers don't need to be following signs. Once the first-responder believers take hold of these
truths and start acting on them, it will provoke others to jealousy
and they will begin to move out in the supernatural, praying for
the sick and sharing words of encouragement and prophecy the
Lord gives them. His Word will not return void (Isaiah 55:11). It's
not possible for you to teach it and plant it in people's hearts and it
not bear fruit.

Make sure to use plenty of illustrations from the Bible, your personal life, and other men and women of God who were used in the gifts. This will also produce faith and hope in people so they can walk in these things as well.

Model and demonstrate the gifts.

In the first Spirit-filled church my wife and I joined, the gifts of the Spirit were demonstrated in most of the services. Though the gifts were in operation, the pastor and leaders did not provide much explanation about the demonstrations we observed. I learned more about them in our Sunday school class and by asking questions of various leaders in the church. I also read several books about the gifts.

Two years later we began attending Lakewood Church in Houston, Texas, where John Osteen was the pastor. At that time there were about 4,000 members in this church. Even in this large church, Brother Osteen would allow the gifts to function. He had two microphones at the front of the church for anyone who had a word to share. He also would stop in the middle of his message at times and give a word to someone in the congregation. He would also teach frequently about the importance of the Baptism in the Holy Spirit and they would pray for the sick in each service. He modeled a good balance of the ministry of the Word and the release of the gifts of the Spirit for me and other growing leaders. I was impacted greatly by this wonderful Spirit-filled pastor who allowed the Spirit to have His way in a larger church.

When I started pastoring, I determined to follow Brother Osteen's example of providing a healthy balance of both the Word and the Spirit. We also gave opportunity for those who needed healing to be prayed for in every service. This type of ministry produced much fruit in our church and the lives of our people. I would pray and prepare messages the Lord gave to me. My worship leader, leadership team, and I would pray together before each service. We simply yielded ourselves to the Spirit and let Him know He could have His way. If He prompted any of us that He wanted to say or do something in the service, we would change our plans and follow Him.

Yielding to the Spirit.

The results of this kind of yielding to the Spirit was remarkable. There was someone being saved, healed, delivered, or ministered to by the Spirit in every service. Sometimes it would occur during the worship. Other times during the ministry of the Word. He would also move powerfully at the end of a service during an altar call or prayer ministry. This kind of balanced ministry of the Word and the Spirit creates a great expectancy in the hearts of the people. And it makes your church and ministry attractive to people hungry for the ministry of the Word and the supernatural.

One example I will share with you happened while I was ministering the Word one Sunday morning. I was about two-thirds through my message when I noticed an interracial couple walk into the service and sit down in the back row. I started to go to my last point and my notes became blurry. I could no longer read them. The letters were all jumbled together and a light mist was over them. Then I tried to read my Bible and the same thing happened. The letters were all jumbled together and a mist was over it. I took off my glasses to make sure it wasn't something to do with my eyes. It was the same thing. I couldn't read anything from either my notes or my Bible.

I could have said a few words from my head and closed the service, but a thought came to me to ask the people to lift their hands and praise God with me for a moment. I was doing that to take time to connect with the Holy Spirit and find out if this was from Him and what He wanted me to do. As we were praising the Lord, I heard the Spirit say to me, "Pray for the couple who just walked in and are sitting in the back." I didn't have anything to lose because I still could not read my notes or my Bible. So I asked that couple if they would mind if we prayed for them. I asked them to stand and also asked one or two church members to stand with them and help me pray for them.

As I began to pray for them, the Lord gave me a word for the man. He was a tall, handsome African American gentleman in his thirties. I told him he was a prince in the kingdom and he had parents who had been praying for him. I let him know his potential was awesome; but in order to fulfill it, he needed to change paths, and in some cases, change some relationships and God would bring him into great success. He started shaking uncontrollably about halfway into the word I gave him. He kept shaking and shaking even after I finished giving him that word.

Then the Lord gave me a word for his companion. I told her, "The Lord knows you have lost something very precious to you, and if you will give your life to Jesus, He will restore everything you have lost and will give you a second chance." She fell in a heap on the floor and began to sob uncontrollably. Well, as you can imagine, my message was over, but the service had really just begun. Our people gathered around this couple and ministered to them for close to an hour. What we found out later was they were both hard-core heroin users. They woke up that morning after almost over-dosing and said to each other, "We need to give God one more chance in our lives."

They had seen the billboard sign that advertised our church on the highway and it took them forty-five minutes to find us. His name was Alvin and her name was Sharon. Alvin had received the

Lord in a Baptist church when he was a boy. His dad was a Baptist deacon who had been praying for him for many years. Alvin had been in a lifestyle of drugs and substance abuse for more than fifteen years. Sharon had not received the Lord until that day. She let our ladies know, who were ministering to her, that she had lost custody of her daughter, Cheri, because of her drug use. God read their mail through the gifts of the Spirit that day.

Alvin and Sharon were married a few weeks later and both became disciples of the Lord. They became the greatest evangelists in our church. They brought more people to Jesus than anyone in all the twenty-four years I served as pastor. One year later, Cheri was placed back in their custody. Praise God. They both got good jobs and became wonderful parents and lived a life that glorified the Lord. What an awesome testimony.

It wasn't my great teaching of the Word that set them free but the gifts of the Spirit. I am not making light of the ministry of the Word. They still needed to be taught the Word in order to become freer, maintain their freedom, and grow in the Lord. The bottom line is we need both the ministry of the Word and the Spirit. As we model this in our services, it will encourage people to walk in the supernatural in their personal lives, workplace, and relationships.

Provide opportunities for people to practice the gifts.

When I began to teach each of my children how to drive, we didn't start out on a major highway. I took each to an empty parking lot where there was very little risk of having an accident. Then we graduated to a Wal-Mart parking lot with many cars. Once they proved they could navigate around the parking lots with confidence, I took them to some back roads with sparse traffic. Finally, after they navigated the back roads with success, we launched out onto a major highway.

Operating in the gifts is a lot like learning to drive a car. Typically, it is best to allow people to practice in smaller settings, like home groups, Bible study classes, or in mid-week services. These settings must be safe places where people need not fear being rebuked or condemned if they make a mistake. Leaders must be trained to encourage the people in their use of the gifts. I have done this in both small and large settings.

I let the group know we are going to practice our operation of the gifts. I will then have them pray in the Spirit quietly for a few minutes, then get in groups of three to five people and release whatever encouragement, Scripture verse, or word the Lord impressed them with for that person while they were praying. The results are always phenomenal. Of course, not every person will share a word or Scripture, but most do and it provides them low-risk opportunities to operate in the gifts. The more opportunities like this you can provide for the people, the more confident they will become in releasing the gifts in larger settings later. It will also produce confidence in them in their ministry to others on a one-on-one basis.

One of the best ways I have discovered to activate people in the gifts is first to teach them for a few minutes on the different flows of the Spirit I shared earlier in this book. Once people understand the flow of love, light, and life and cooperate with that, the gifts always manifest. Whenever I teach on this for fifteen to twenty minutes to any size group and then have them spend a few minutes in prayer, it never fails that the gifts start flowing through individuals.

Love, respect, and value each member of the body.

Many churches are famous for recognizing and platforming the super-gifted and talented members of the body. Those talented musicians, singers, or artists who can bring immediate benefit to the ministry of the local church seem to receive an inordinate amount of attention and respect by church leaders compared to the average, everyday faithful member of the church. This might help fill the immediate hole in the worship team talent pool, but it does not promote the release of the gifts in the body. The gifts have their highest degree of expression through an atmosphere of mutual love, respect, and value of all members of the body.

Paul deals with this enemy of member comparison in First Corinthians chapter 12:

> If the foot should say, "Because I am not a hand, I am not of the body," is it therefore not of the body? And if the ear should say, "Because I am not an eye, I am not of the body," is it therefore not of the body?" (1 Corinthians 12:15-16).

Why would the foot want to be the hand and the ear covet to be the eye in the body? What is the primary difference in the relative value of each member of the body? Is the hand more significant than the foot or the eye more important than the ear? Each member is significant. What is the primary distinction between the hand and foot and the eye and ear besides their specific function? It is *visibility*. You see a person's eye first and most more than the ear. And you see someone's hand more than you notice the foot.

That is the primary challenge in the Lord's spiritual body today. Everyone wants to be noticed in order to feel valued. Therefore, people will fight to sing in the worship team because they are on the platform, but most children's ministries have to beg people to help them in their ministry. Everyone wants to be the quarterback or running back on the football team. But the body of Christ doesn't function that way, and the gifts of the Spirit don't flow best that way. We can't all be quarterbacks and platform people. Find your place in the body and function there with humility and thankfulness.

God sets each one of us in the body where it pleases Him (1 Corinthians 12:18). It should please us to function in the body where it pleases Him. Ask God where you fit, follow your desires, and ask yourself, *Where do I sense God's pleasure when I serve and where are people blessed most when I serve?*

> *And the eye cannot say to the hand, "I have no need of you"; nor again the head to the feet, "I have no need of you"* (1 Corinthians 12:21).

Who is the head of the body? Jesus! As the head, Jesus cannot even say to the lowest part of the body, the feet, "I have no need of you!" There are no insignificant, second-class, or unneeded members in the body. It is incumbent upon leaders in the church to be intentional about noticing, valuing, and publicly praising members who are not as visible as others.

I did this intentionally in my church. Once or twice per month I would recognize members who were ministering life and the Word to others behind the scenes. I would either call them on stage or have them stand up and then read or tell the testimony of someone who had received the benefit of their ministry. Whatever you praise publicly, you will release and reap in the body behind the scenes. As we show love and value in tangible ways to the less visible members of the body, it will encourage other members to step out in ministry to others.

I speak a word of grace—divine enablement—over you as you apply these principles to create a healthy environment of the supernatural and the release of the gifts of the Spirit in your small group, church, and ministry.

Chapter 18

HE WILL SHOW US THINGS TO COME

A GOOD FRIEND OF MINE, ROY, SHARED AN INTERESTING EVENT with me that happened to him a couple of years ago at Mardi Gras in New Orleans. Roy and some close friends had been going annually with a nationally known ministry for several years to share the gospel with those attending Mardi Gras. This year he and his team were walking down Bourbon Street and they came upon a woman standing outside a storefront that had a banner above the door: "Palm Reading." As Roy and one of his team stopped to minister to her, she asked him, "Do you want to know your future?" Roy's answer was classic. He told her, "I know my future. Would you like to know yours?" He went on to tell her, "I found my future reading the Psalms, not by anyone reading my palms!"

Roy then shared the gospel and the love of Jesus with her. He also gave her a word of knowledge the Holy Spirit showed him about her that brought her to tears. Though she didn't immediately accept the Lord, they planted a good seed in her heart. The next day he and his team came up with a "God idea" from their divine appointment with this lady. They brought a card table and a chair and set up on a sidewalk with a sign on the front of the table: "Free Psalm Reading." Dozens of people stopped by that day with whom they shared the gospel and gave many words of knowledge and words of wisdom regarding their lives and God's plan for them. Dozens of people were saved that day because people stopped who were curious about their future.

The truth is, God knows our future. He has a perfect plan for our lives but He does not force it on us.

> *Your eyes saw my substance, being yet unformed. And in Your book they all were written, the days fashioned for me, when as yet there were none of them. How precious also are Your thoughts to me, O God! How great is the sum of them!* (Psalm 139:16-17)

> *For I know the thoughts that I think toward you, says the Lord, thoughts of peace and not of evil, to give you a future and a hope* (Jeremiah 29:11).

These are two powerful passages of Scripture that clearly state God has a good future planned for each of us. He has established this future and good plan for our lives before we were born. This plan includes peace, prosperity, and success, not evil and calamity! If that is the case, why then do so many struggle in life to find the peace, prosperity, and success He promises are a part of His plan and thoughts for us? The reason is very simple. So many of His children live their lives in light of their own plan for themselves instead of seeking Him to discover His plan for their lives. This is born out in the following two verses of Jeremiah chapter 29:

> *Then you will call upon Me and go and pray to Me, and I will listen to you. And you will seek Me and find Me, when you search for Me with all your heart* (Jeremiah 29:12-13).

He follows His promise to us in verse 11 of a good future for our lives with the means to enter into that future—by praying and seeking Him. *The will and plan of God for our lives must be discovered, not decided!* And we discover our future—His will and plan for our lives—by seeking Him. This is not a one-time, random kind of seeking God. This involves living a life of continually seeking Him, looking to Him, yielding to Him, depending on Him, and following Him as He leads us. God knows the future and plans He has for you and me. Discovering our future requires our heart and mind going after Him and His will for our lives. He has hidden His will and plan for us, not from us. He delights to show us the future He has for us inside our relationship with Him as we seek Him.

Just before Jesus left His disciples, He shared an important principle with them regarding the place of the Holy Spirit in their lives.

> *I still have many things to say to you, but you cannot bear them now. However, when He, the Spirit of truth, has come, He will guide you into all truth; for He will not speak on His own authority, but whatever He hears He will speak; and He will tell you things to come* (John 16:12-13).

The last part of this verse in the King James version of the Bible says, *"He will shew [show] you things to come."* One major aspect of the ministry of the Holy Spirit is to show us our future! Since this is true, it is imperative we develop a personal relationship with the Holy Spirit. Since my wife and I were filled with the Spirit in 1976, our revelation and understanding of God's plan for our lives has been continually unfolding. And our personal relationship with the Holy Spirit has grown immensely.

For the past forty-plus years we have embarked on an incredible journey of discovering and walking out God's future and plan for us. The fruit of this has been nothing less than supernatural. We have experienced God's peace, prosperity, and hope in our lives just as Jeremiah 29 promises. We also have walked in a supernatural ministry that has brought healing, encouragement, and life to many.

The Holy Spirit can show us things about our future in many ways. It can come in a dream or a vision. It can also come while you are reading the Word or hearing the Word taught by someone. He can speak to us through an impression, an inward witness, or an inward desire He plants in our hearts. He can also speak to us through one of the gifts of the Spirit such as prophecy or a word of wisdom. These are just a few of the ways the Spirit can begin to show us our future, but He is not limited to how He speaks to us.

I want to reiterate something I shared earlier in this book. A word of wisdom through a prophetic word regarding our future is not automatic. It is usually conditional based on the response of the recipient of the word. The way I have heard a prophet friend of mine describe it is, "A prophetic word is a divine invitation into your kingdom potential." It is our responsibility to test that word by the Word of God, mature leaders we have relationship with, and the witness we have in our hearts (see the chapter "How to Judge a Prophetic Word"). Once you have determined this word has come from the Spirit, you have to mix it with faith, hold on to it, and speak it out until it comes to pass.

In my walk with God and developing my personal relationship with the Spirit, I have discovered He will show us two types of things regarding our future. First, He will show us things regarding our kingdom potential and inheritance. Second, He will show us plans of the enemy that we can either avoid, overcome, or stop. Understanding each of these areas of our future is essential to us walking in God's will and plan for our lives. Let me share with you some personal examples of each of these areas the Holy Spirit will show us things to come.

Our Kingdom Assignment

The first area is our future regarding our kingdom assignment, potential, or inheritance. When I received the Baptism in the Holy Spirit in the spring of 1976, the Spirit led me to spend a lot of time in prayer for my family members who were not yet saved and also about God's plan and future for my life. I observed and heard many testimonies on Christian television and in my new church about the Holy Spirit using normal people in supernatural ways. I began to seek the Lord, asking Him to use me. I owned a very successful wholesale florist company and made lots of money at the time. Yet there was a growing dissatisfaction in my heart regarding the will of God.

In the summer of 1976 I had scheduled a fishing trip in the remote northern part of Canada with my dad, grandfather, and my brother. While on this trip I had a lot of extra time to spend reading the Word. One day while I was reading in the first chapter of Luke, the Holy Spirit stopped me and highlighted two phrases from two separate verses and impressed me strongly this was the future and plan He had prepared for me. The following are those two verses and the portions He highlighted to me:

*Just as those who from the beginning were eyewitnesses and **ministers of the word** delivered them to us* (Luke 1:2).

*He will also go before Him in the spirit and power of Elijah, "to turn the hearts of the fathers to the children," and the disobedient to the wisdom of the just, **to make ready a people prepared for the Lord*** (Luke 1:17).

I had been seeking Him for about three months at the time and this was one of the first things the Spirit revealed to me regarding God's plan for my future. He focused me on two separate phrases from each of these verses and confirmed in my heart that He had called me to be a *minister of the Word to make ready a people prepared for the Lord.* Praise God. I could read those verses a hundred times and never come up with that revelation on my own. Now granted, I didn't see myself as a minister of the Word yet. I saw myself as a successful business man. But I did realize this was the Holy Spirit revealing my future to me even though I didn't fully understand it.

Later that year one morning in October, my wife came to me while I was shaving and announced to me she had heard something clearly from the Lord. I hesitantly asked her to share it with me. She told me God had just spoken to her in prayer and told her she was a pastor's wife.

At that time, I had been evangelizing with a small group of people from our church on the streets of downtown Houston, Texas. We had asked many of the people from our church to go with us but very few responded. As a result, I had made some judgments about the church and one of those was I would never be a pastor because the people in the church are so passive and lazy.

Those judgments caused me to react in a negative way to my wife's wonderful news from the Lord. I told her, "Well if God spoke that to you, that means one of three things. One, I'm going to die and you are going to marry a pastor. Two, we are going to get a divorce and you will marry a pastor. And three, God is going to have to change my heart because I don't want anything to do with those lazy, good-for-nothing saints!" You have to understand I was very young and immature at the time and my response caused my wife to cry and go off and question whether she had heard from God or not. Yet I am confident, looking back, this was another clear word from the Holy Spirit regarding the future He had planned for us.

About six months later after a night of evangelism on the streets of downtown Houston, I came home and was seeking the Lord because of a lingering dissatisfaction in my heart. I knelt down next to my living room couch and began to pray in the Spirit. My heart was crying out, wondering what this lingering dissatisfaction was about. After praying in the Spirit for about thirty minutes, I stopped and decided to listen. Immediately I heard the Spirit say very clearly to me, "I have called you to equip the saints."

This startled me because my heart had been for evangelism. At the same time the Spirit reminded me of what He had revealed to me while I was on that fishing trip in Canada and what He had spoken to my wife back in the fall. He was confirming in my heart He had indeed called me to be a pastor and teacher who would equip the saints. I also did not understand clearly what "equipping the saints" meant in entirety. But He did let me know that pastoring people and evangelism were not mutually exclusive. They actually go together as we see in the book of Acts. I also knew from what He revealed to me the year before, I would be involved in ministering the Word to make ready a people prepared for the Lord.

Seeking the Lord

From this direction I began to seek the Lord about the possibility of going to Bible college somewhere. I actually applied to the Bible college I eventually attended, but they were full at the time. I spent a lot of time studying the Word and continued running my business for the next two years. We had moved to Lakewood Church in Houston, Texas, where John Osteen was the pastor at this time and we continued growing in our knowledge of the Word. Then one day while counting money and checks from my business preparing for a bank deposit, I heard in my head that old Peggy Lee song, "Is that all there is?"

I knew from this, God had more for my life than just making money and business. I knew in my spirit He wanted me to go to Bible college to prepare for the ministry He was calling me to—the one He had planned all along for my future. This time I applied to Rhema Bible Training Center in Broken Arrow, Oklahoma, was accepted, and spent the next two years preparing for His call on our lives. We subsequently pastored two churches for twenty-seven years.

I am now pastoring pastors and leaders in my role at Charis Bible College in Woodland Park, Colorado, as well as traveling and teaching in churches and Bible colleges throughout the U.S. and the world. I can truly say after all these years that discovering and following the will and plan of God for my life—my future—has been the most fulfilling time of our lives. He has a similar plan and future for you. As you seek Him you will discover it and find the same fulfillment He has brought to us.

The Plans of the Enemy

The second area the Holy Spirit will show us things to come is regarding the plans of the enemy for our lives. Do you remember hearing about the tsunami in Sri Lanka several years ago? Following a large earthquake in the ocean off the coast of Sri Lanka, a giant wave formed and brought devastation to the low coastal areas of that country. Many buildings were destroyed and lives were lost. Our church actually sent a medical team into that area to help the survivors. The reports that came back to us from the missionaries in that region were very interesting.

They shared two things I have never forgotten. First, many of the animals in the lower coastal areas followed their instinct and fled to higher ground ahead of the tsunami. Second, many people they knew, especially Christians, had an urgent sense they needed to leave that area ahead of the tsunami and their lives were spared. The point is, if animals can follow their instinct and go to higher ground ahead of a tsunami, then Christians can follow the inward warnings from the Holy Spirit and flee to higher ground ahead of impending danger!

On 9/11/2001, approximately 3,000 people lost their lives. That was a major national catastrophe we will never forget. There were many interesting stories individuals shared following this event. The Twin Towers' office capacity was approximately 30,000 people, yet only 3,000 or 10 percent of those perished. And of those 3,000, many who lost their lives were hundreds of first responders. Of course, many fled who were able after the first attack on the first tower. Yet, scores of testimonies from people who were officed there were very similar.

"Something was telling me not to go to work today." Or, "For some unknown reason I just felt like I needed to stop by and pick up my cleaning," or "I just felt like I needed to stop by the coffee shop and go in late that day." Many others felt a need to take a sick day and not go in.

Then there were the four planes that went down. One of those planes only had sixteen passengers. When have you ever been on a plane that seats one hundred and thirty people take off with only sixteen passengers? What happened on that fateful day? I believe the Holy Spirit was warning many people to avoid the evil and danger that was about to happen. No doubt He was trying to warn all who were in the path of this impending danger and some people listened, followed their hearts, and their lives were spared.

Some call this following "women's intuition." The reason I believe it is labeled this way is because women typically will follow their hearts more readily than men. Many times men will allow reason to take over when the Holy Spirit is trying to speak to them in their spirit, where He resides in those who are born again.

I have done a personal survey of all those I know who lived through a tragic accident or some other calamity that resulted in physical harm to them or one of their family members. I have asked dozens of people who have gone through things like this, "Was there anything going on in your heart just prior to that accident or calamity that was telling you to wait or not go there?" Over 95 percent of those I surveyed told me that something was telling them not to leave or not to go to that place where the accident or calamity happened. Have you ever been in a place you knew in your heart you weren't supposed to be? Have you ever had something in your heart urge you not to leave on that trip or urge you to leave the place you are right then? That is most likely the Holy Spirit warning you and attempting to lead you away from some evil plan of the enemy to hurt or harm you or someone you love.

Anytime you get that sense in your spirit of some impending danger where you are planning on going or you are in the wrong place, I encourage you to follow the leading of the Spirit. His leading will always bring peace with it. My experience is, the more inclined I am to follow my reasoning and press on in spite of what the Spirit is telling me in my heart, the less peace I will have. Look at the following verse with me:

A prudent man foresees the evil and hides himself, but the simple pass on and are punished (Proverbs 22:3).

How can we foresee the evil plans of the enemy and hide ourselves? That is simple. We just need to remain sensitive to the Holy Spirit and be willing to follow His leading in our hearts instead of pressing on and following the leading of our minds. This verse tells us if we fail to do that and just press on following our reasoning, we will be punished. This is not punishment from the Lord. Rather it is punishment by the enemy of our souls.

Several years ago during a time of prayer, my wife and I had this foreboding sense that the enemy was attempting to bring some type of hurt or harm to someone in our family. While we were praying in the Spirit, the Lord showed my wife a vision of a red pickup truck driving fast down the street and our son, Michael, running into the street in front of it. Michael was three years old at the time of this vision. We took authority over the spirit of death and bound the enemy off of Michael and declared the Word over him:

No evil shall befall you, nor shall any plague come near your dwelling; for He shall give His angels charge over you, to keep you in all your ways (Psalm 91:10-11).

We spent a good deal of time after that praising God that Michael was safe and angels were given charge over him to keep him in all his ways! After a time, that strong sense of impending danger lifted and God's peace and joy filled our hearts. Of course, we also were careful after that to ensure Michael did not go near any street. Two years later, my family and I had taken a few days off to go to the beach in Galveston, Texas. Our two older sons, Brian who was seven, and Michael, who was five, asked to go to the beach.

We decided that Janice would take the boys and our infant daughter, Michelle, to the beach for a short time while I stayed back at the hotel to finish preparing a message for the church I pastored the following Sunday. As my family crossed the street to go to the beach, they stopped on the median to wait for the oncoming traffic on the other side of the road to pass. My son, Michael, thinking Janice was continuing across the street ran out ahead of her. When Janice noticed Michael had run out in the street, she looked to the right and there was the red pickup truck she had seen in that vision two years earlier. She screamed, "Michael!" and he supernaturally flew backward into her arms.

Praise God. This had to be the work of an angel we had prayed over Michael two years before. The enemy had plans to take Michael's life but the Holy Spirit showed us those plans in advance. We had already taken care of this by the leading of the Spirit and the enemy's evil plan was thwarted! He will show us things to come; and if we will follow His leading, there is nothing the enemy can do that will stop our destiny and future!

Another time during a time of prayer before I took the children to school one day I felt like something was wrong in my spirit and I began to pray in the Spirit. I took authority over the enemy, bound the spirit of death off of my family, and continued to pray. I told my wife something was wrong and I could not take the children to school at that time. She informed them to wait, they may not be going to school that day and they all cheered. I kept praying for thirty minutes more and all of a sudden God's peace came in my heart and I knew all was well.

I told Janice to tell the boys to get ready, that I was going to take them to school now. They both chimed in unison, "Oh, Dad!"

They weren't happy I had changed my mind and now was taking them to school about forty-five minutes late. As we drove the normal route to their school, we came to I45 in Houston, Texas, and started to get on the freeway but could not because there was an eighteen-car pileup that had occurred forty-five minutes before because of a heavy fog that morning. We could have been involved in that but were not because the Holy Spirit showed us ahead of time to avoid that impending danger!

I will share one final example with you of the Holy Spirit showing us things to come to avoid the evil plans of the enemy. A good friend of mine, Paul Milligan who is the CEO of Andrew Wommack Ministries, was an elder in my church for twenty-four years. In 1989 he had just started his first business and every potential client was valuable. He was scheduled to fly to San Francisco in October of that year to sign a deal with one of the largest clients he had to date. He woke up that morning and felt in his heart something was wrong. As he was driving to the airport, he began to pray in the Spirit, asking the Holy Spirit to show him what was wrong.

He didn't hear anything specific, except he knew he could not get on the plane to San Francisco that day. Something in his heart was telling him there was danger and harm ahead. He finally called his secretary and told her to call and cancel his appointment with that client. He had cancelled with this client once before so this did not seem to be the reasonable thing to do. She called and canceled the appointment and thankfully was able to reschedule. The Paul Harvey's "rest of the story"—this was the day of the huge earthquake in the San Francisco Bay area. And the bridge that collapsed was the bridge Paul would have been traveling on at approximately the same time it actually collapsed.

Praise God for the Holy Spirit. He will show us things to come. He will show us our future and His plans for our lives. He will also show us at times the enemy's plans so we can avoid them, overcome them, and stop them. Thank God we have the person of the Holy Spirit who knows everything and will help us move into our future with abundance, peace, and success. He will also lead us to avert danger, calamity and evil if we will listen to and follow Him.

Chapter 19

THE BAPTISM IN THE SPIRIT IS THE DOORWAY TO THE SUPERNATURAL

I WAS BORN AGAIN ON EASTER SUNDAY IN 1973 IN A METHODIST church from the Word I had heard seven to eight years earlier in a Baptist church. I was very thankful for that born-again experience, knowing my sins were all forgiven and I was going to Heaven. But I had no clue I was righteous in my spirit or that I could have a personal relationship with the Holy Spirit. In fact, I didn't even know who the Holy Spirit was.

Each Sunday in our church they would sing the Doxology at the end of each service. The lyrics say, "Praise God, from whom all blessings flow, praise Him, all creatures here below; praise Him above, ye heavenly host; praise Father, Son, and Holy Ghost."

When we got to the last phrase I would say, "Praise Father, Son and *Holy Who?*" I had never been taught about the Holy Spirit and wondered to myself, who is He and what is His part in the Godhead? It was only when I was filled with the Spirit in 1976 and began attending a Spirit-filled church that I began to understand the significance of His place in my life. Prior to that time, I was completely ignorant regarding the Holy Spirit, the gifts of the Spirit, and the supernatural power of God available to each of us.

What I discovered from the Word and from my experience in receiving the Holy Spirit is *the Baptism in the Spirit is the doorway to the gifts and the supernatural in our lives!* Before I was filled with the Spirit there were zero gifts of the Spirit and no supernatural flowing through my life. After I received the Baptism in the Spirit, all of the gifts of the Spirit and the supernatural were available to me and operated through me.

This created a major transformation in my life. My relationship with God grew by leaps and bounds. I was able to overcome temptation and sin that had ruled my life up to that point, even as a Christian. I was now experiencing the book of Acts instead of just reading about it and praying for it in my life! All of a sudden, the Bible, which had been a dark book to me, came alive with revelation and understanding. This is all confirmed in the following verses:

> ...*Surely I will pour out my Spirit on you; I will make my words known to you* (Proverbs 1:23).

> *Now we have received, not the spirit of the world, but the Spirit who is from God, that we might know the things that have been freely given to us by God* (1 Corinthians 2:12).

The Spirit has been given to us to reveal the Word to us and to help us know the things that have been freely given to us by God.

The Holy Spirit is the Author of the Word. Therefore, He is the one most qualified to reveal the truth to us and give us understanding of the Word He inspired.

> *But the Helper, the Holy Spirit, whom the Father will send in My name, He will teach you all things, and bring to your remembrance all things that I said to you* (John 14:26).

Isn't the Word enough for us? Yes, the Word is enough for us, but we just read in the Word in John chapter 14 each of us needs the ministry of the Holy Spirit to teach us. Even Jesus, the living Word, who had the Bible, the Old Testament Scriptures, was still filled with the Spirit.

> *When He had been baptized, Jesus came up immediately from the water; and behold, the heavens were opened to Him, and He saw the Spirit of God descending like a dove and alighting upon Him* (Matthew 3:16).

If Jesus needed to be filled with the Spirit, you and I need to be filled with the Spirit. Aren't we filled with the Spirit at the new birth? We do receive the Spirit in a measure in the new birth, but there is a subsequent infilling of the Spirit each of us needs to empower us to be witnesses for Him.

In Hebrews chapter 6, the writer describes one of the fundamental doctrines of Christ is the doctrine of baptisms (plural). There are three primary baptisms included in this doctrine of baptisms each believer needs to receive to align themselves to the doctrine of Christ.

The first baptism is *the baptism by the Spirit into the body of Christ at the new birth*. The following verse describes this essential baptism:

> *For by one Spirit we were all baptized into one body—*
> *whether Jews or Greeks, whether slaves or free—and have*
> *all been made to drink into one Spirit* (1 Corinthians
> 12:13).

Notice the agent of this baptism: *"by one Spirit we were all baptized...."* This baptism takes place at the new birth. The Spirit baptizes us into the body of Christ when we received Jesus as our Lord and Savior! This is not the same baptism as the baptism into the Spirit we will see later. This is the baptism into the body of Christ by the Spirit. With each of these three baptisms there is a different agent who does the baptizing.

The second baptism is *water baptism*. This baptism can only be legitimate after one is born again and baptized into the body of Christ by the Spirit. We see this baptism described in the following verse:

> *Go therefore and make disciples of all the nations, baptiz-*
> *ing them in the name of the Father and of the Son and of*
> *the Holy Spirit* (Matthew 28:19).

The agent of this baptism is you and me or some other human agent. This baptism is the funeral service for the old man. When we are born again, our old man has died and we receive the nature of Christ. We are brand-new in our spirit. We don't have a good dog and a bad dog inside us fighting against each other. The bad dog was run over by the cross! Whenever we are immersed in water baptism, we are identifying with our new identity in Christ and acknowledging our old man and nature has died.

The third baptism is the *baptism into the Spirit by Jesus*. This is the baptism where we are filled with the Spirit that opens up our understanding of the Word and opens us up to operate in the gifts and the supernatural power of God. This baptism is found in the following verse:

> *I indeed baptize you with water unto repentance, but He who is coming after me is mightier than I, whose sandals I am not worthy to carry. He will baptize you with the Holy Spirit and fire* (Matthew 3:11).

Notice the agent of this baptism is Jesus, not the Spirit. In this baptism, Jesus baptizes us into the Holy Spirit and we are filled with the Spirit. We have the Spirit in the new birth prior to this baptism. But this baptism is subsequent to salvation. In this baptism, Jesus immerses us into the Holy Spirit. Jesus tells us this baptism can only be received after someone is born again and becomes a child of God.

> *If you then, being evil, know how to give good gifts to your children, how much more will your heavenly Father give the Holy Spirit to those who ask Him!* (Luke 11:13)

The context of this verse in Luke 11 is a son asking his father for something. The specific example Jesus uses here is a child of God asking the Father for the Holy Spirit. If we received all of the Spirit we needed at the new birth, why then would Jesus instruct born-again children of God to ask their Father for the Holy Spirit they already have in His fullness? This third baptism can only be received by born-again children of God, therefore is always subsequent to salvation. A lost person can ask and receive Jesus but cannot ask for this baptism into the Spirit until he or she is born again.

The apostle John makes a clear distinction between these two baptisms. He uses the analogy of different types of water to compare this to two different baptisms and internal works of the Spirit.

But whosoever drinketh of the water that I shall give him shall never thirst; but the water that I shall give him shall be in him a **well of water** *springing up into everlasting life* (John 4:14 KJV).

In the last day, that great day of the feast, Jesus stood and cried, saying, If any man thirst, let him come unto me, and drink. He that believeth on me, as the scripture hath said, out of his belly shall flow **rivers of living water.** *(But this spake he of the Spirit, which they that believe on him should receive: for the Holy Ghost was not yet given; because that Jesus was not yet glorified.)* (John 7:37-39 KJV).

The verse in John chapter 4 describes the work of the Spirit in the new birth. Notice he describes this as a *well of water* in a person when they receive everlasting life at the new birth. The passage in John chapter 7 speaks of the baptism in the Spirit. Notice in this passage he describes it as *rivers of living water* flowing out of us as opposed to a well of water in us.

He also says this is for those who believe on Him first. He goes on to say those who believe on Him should also receive this baptism and work of the Spirit. The results will be the Spirit flowing out of us as rivers of living water. He is speaking in this passage of the Baptism in the Holy Spirit. This baptism opens the door to the supernatural and the operation of the gifts flowing through us.

Jesus told His disciples not to go out without this essential baptism.

And being assembled together with them, He commanded them not to depart from Jerusalem, but to wait for the Promise of the Father, "which," He said, "you have heard from Me: for John truly baptized with water, but you shall be baptized with the Holy Spirit not many days from now" (Acts 1:4-5).

But you shall receive power when the Holy Spirit has come upon you; and you shall be witnesses to Me in Jerusalem, and in all Judea, and Samaria, and to the end of the earth (Acts 1:8).

Behold, I send the Promise of My Father upon you; but tarry in the city of Jerusalem until you are endued with power from on high (Luke 24:49).

This was not something optional for Jesus' disciples. According to Jesus, receiving the Baptism in the Holy Spirit is what empowered them to be witnesses of Him and to do His works. This Baptism in the Spirit is for all believers. It equips us to be more sensitive to Him, to operate the gifts in confidence, and to become true witnesses of Jesus' life and ministry.

On the day of Pentecost, one hundred and twenty of His disciples did indeed wait in an upper room in prayer for this baptism. And they all received the Baptism in the Spirit. The results were Peter was transformed from a coward to one who preached the Word in power and anointing. Three thousand people gave their lives to the Lord that day! All because of this Baptism in the Spirit they had just received.

Another evidence or character trait of this baptism by Jesus into the Spirit was they all received a new spiritual language the Bible calls speaking with other tongues.

And they were all filled with the Holy Spirit and began to speak with other tongues, as the Spirit gave them utterance (Acts 2:4).

Some people get nervous when there is talk about the evidence of being filled with the Spirit is speaking with other tongues. Yet it is in the Bible. And it was one of the primary evidences the early church was filled with the Spirit. It is still an essential evidence of someone being filled with the Spirit today. Why did God choose tongues as an evidence of being full of the Spirit? Because the tongue is one of our most unruly members. And when we are willing to yield our tongue and lips to speak a language our mind cannot control, it is a sign or evidence we are completely yielded to and filled with the Spirit.

After I received the baptism in the Spirit with the evidence of speaking with other tongues, I had some Christian friends come to me and express concern about this experience. They were from a denomination that taught against tongues. One individual pleaded with me to stay away from things like this because it could open the door to the devil. They had never expressed any concern about my walk with the Lord previously. I told them this was in the Bible. I asked them how was it possible that acting on something in the Bible could open me up to the devil? I went on to tell them since I was filled with the Spirit and prayed in other tongues, I understood the Bible better, was more in love with Jesus and walking closer to Jesus than I had ever been in my Christian life.

I asked them how something that was in the Bible that had drawn me closer to the Lord, and helped me understand the Word better could possibly be of the devil? They had no answer except to say, "Just be careful with all this tongues business." I didn't argue with them anymore. I understand when someone has been taught against something it is difficult to readily embrace it. Whatever people are not "up on" they are usually "down on."

But this Baptism in the Spirit had radically changed my life and opened me up to the supernatural flowing through my life. I know how I lived prior to being filled with the Spirit and that was a dead, dull spiritual life, with no power and little spiritual understanding in my life. This baptism in the Spirit is a doorway into the supernatural and is for every believer. I believe another reason God chose tongues as the primary evidence of being filled with the Spirit is because tongues is a pride buster. Tongues is typically looked down upon by modern-day Pharisees in many denominational churches. It is neither rational, acceptable, or proper among "dignified" Christians.

I am not interested in pleasing people by acting dignified according others' religious standards. I will just stick with the Word of God. *I will stand by the truth no matter who that separates me from or connects me with.* I am not ashamed of the gospel. I am not ashamed of the Holy Spirit, and I am not ashamed to declare I am filled with the Spirit and pray regularly in other tongues.

God is not interested in wounding our pride. He wants to kill it. I am not going to allow pride to stop me from receiving the blessings God has promised me, including the fullness of the Spirit!

This Baptism in the Spirit is for you today:

> *Then Peter said to them, "Repent, and let every one of you be baptized in the name of Jesus Christ for the remission of sins; and you shall receive the gift of the Holy Spirit. For the promise is to you and to your children, and to all who are afar off, as many as the Lord our God will call"* (Acts 2:38-39).

Let me ask you a simple question. Have you been filled with the Spirit with the evidence of speaking in other tongues since you have believed? If not, you can receive this essential baptism today. All that is necessary is for you to simply ask for it. Let me lead you in a simple prayer right now.

"Father, I thank You for the gift of salvation I received when I accepted Jesus as my Lord and Savior. When I received Jesus, the Spirit baptized me into the body of Christ, making me a member of Christ's body, and I thank You for that. But I see in Your Word there is another baptism you have for me. That is the baptism into the Spirit with the evidence of speaking with other tongues. I am asking You to fill me with the Spirit. I receive the fullness of the Spirit right now with the evidence of speaking in other tongues in Jesus' name. Amen."

Now I want to encourage you to lift your hands and heart to the Lord and thank Him for filling you with the Holy Spirit. Next I want to encourage you to stop speaking in your native language and begin to speak whatever sound or syllable comes to your mind that is not a language you are familiar with. In Acts 2:4 it says they *began to speak with other tongues.* They spoke in tongues. The Holy Spirit did not speak with tongues. They did. And He doesn't move our lips and tongue to speak. You have to lend your voice to the Holy Spirit and begin to speak.

If you prayed that prayer, I believe you have been filled with the Spirit. You have been baptized into the Spirit, and you will speak with other tongues as a new spiritual language.

In the following chapter, I share about the benefits of praying in other tongues. You are embarking on an amazing new spiritual journey that is full of revelation and supernatural encounters you have only read about until now. I would love for you to write me if you have received the Baptism in the Holy Spirit with the evidence of speaking with other tongues and how it has impacted your life.

Chapter 20

THE BENEFITS OF PRAYING IN TONGUES

THE SUBJECT OF TONGUES HAS BEEN A POINT OF CONTENTION between many sincere Christians. Some people are simply afraid of tongues because they have been taught against it. They use First Corinthians 12:30, "...*Do all speak with tongues?*" to teach not all can speak with tongues. They imply tongues is just for a few specialized saints. The truth is, Paul was not addressing the gift of tongues that anyone can receive who is filled with the Spirit here. He was addressing those who have been called to a ministry office equipped with the gift of tongues and interpretation of tongues. Not all will function in a ministry office with these gifts. Yet Paul says in First Corinthians 14:5, "*I wish you all spoke with tongues....*"

Still others teach that tongues will cease from First Corinthians 13:8. These same teachers also typically teach the gifts passed away when the New Testament canon of Scripture arrived. They say the Bible is that which is perfect to come. If that were true, why would the Holy Spirit inspire Paul to pen First Corinthians chapter 14 regarding the proper biblical order of the operation of the gifts if they would pass away as soon as they received the New Testament canon of Scripture? That just doesn't make sense. No, tongues and the other gifts will not cease or pass away until that which is perfect returns and we see Him—Jesus—face to face! I provide a more complete answer to both of these questions in the latter part of Chapter 6 in this book.

There are others who won't open their hearts to the truth about the blessing of this new spiritual language, tongues, God has for us because they don't want to be identified with fanatics. Yet the same people aren't concerned at all about being a fanatic at their home team's baseball or football game or at their son's soccer game or their daughter's basketball game.

The truth is, most of us are fanatical about something we really value. I have decided to be a fanatic for Jesus and His Word. Tongues, a new spiritual language, is in the Word and the evidence God chose to indicate someone is filled with the Spirit. Therefore, I have chosen to embrace it rather than be ashamed of it because it is not the dignified or respectable "high church" thing to do. As I mentioned in the last chapter, I have decided to stick with the Word no matter who it separates me from or who it connects me with.

Our experience of receiving the Baptism in the Holy Spirit with the evidence of speaking with other tongues has been the most significant biblical principle that has launched my wife and I into a supernatural life and ministry. In this chapter I share with you the benefits of praying in other tongues both from the Word and our experience. There are seven major benefits of praying in tongues I have found in the Word.

1. Praying in tongues facilitates your intimacy with God.

For he who speaks in a tongue does not speak to men but to God... (1 Corinthians 14:2).

This verse declares praying in tongues is direct communication with God. It is our spirit communicating directly with His Spirit. The following verse bears this out:

For if I pray in a tongue, my spirit prays... (1 Corinthians 14:14).

Whenever you and I are praying in tongues, it is our spirit that is doing the praying. When we pray with our understanding in the language we are familiar with, our mind and emotions are involved in that prayer. Certainly this kind of prayer is legitimate. It is just limited. It is limited to our understanding, our knowledge of God's Word and God's will. When we are praying in the Spirit, our spirit is speaking to His Spirit. In other words, we are speaking directly to God.

Though our minds don't know what we are praying, God receives it. And because it is spirit to Spirit communication, it causes us to be more sensitive to the person of the Holy Spirit. I have experienced many times of praying in tongues for twenty to thirty minutes or longer. And each time it has drawn me closer to the Lord and caused me to sense and know His love and presence in a much more tangible way than praying in English and running out of words to say.

2. Praying in tongues edifies us.

He who speaks in a tongue edifies himself... (1 Corinthians 14:4).

This may not seem rational but this is exactly what the Word declares. Praying in tongues brings encouragement and strength to our inner man. The Greek word for edify means to encourage, build up, confirm, restore, and establish. There are so many challenges we go through in the Christian life that are designed to discourage us, accuse us, weaken us, and tear us down. The enemy does his best to get our focus on the wrong things in an effort to cause us to quit. Each of us needs daily encouragement from others in the body. We also need to make ourselves available to encourage others in the body daily.

> *Beware, brethren, lest there be in any of you an evil heart of unbelief in departing from the living God; but exhort one another daily, while it is called "Today," lest any of you be hardened through the deceitfulness of sin* (Hebrews 3:12-13).

In order to be in a place to offer encouragement to others, we must do our part to keep ourselves encouraged. Praying in the Spirit does that for us. There have been so many times I have allowed circumstances, actions, or attitudes by people to cause me to consider being discouraged. As I take time to pray in the Spirit, I begin to receive God's perspective on the situation.

When I see things from His viewpoint, everything doesn't look so bad. I am actually encouraged in the midst of circumstances or situations that have not yet been resolved from the natural standpoint. As I receive encouragement from the Lord by praying in the Spirit, I then purpose to be intentionally encouraging to others.

And I will eventually reap what I am sowing. When I am praying in the Spirit, in other tongues, I am actually sowing to the Spirit. What I sow I will reap!

3. Praying in tongues draws up wisdom from your spirit to your mind.

In order to explain this benefit of praying in tongues we need to look at two verses:

> *For he who speaks in a tongue does not speak to men but to God, for no one understands him; however, in the spirit he speaks mysteries* (1 Corinthians 14:2).
>
> *But we speak the wisdom of God in a mystery, the hidden wisdom which God ordained before the ages for our glory* (1 Corinthians 2:7).

The first verse tells us when we are praying in the Spirit we are speaking mysteries. The second verse tells us we speak the wisdom of God in a mystery. When connecting these two verses, we see clearly that praying in other tongues is praying up the wisdom of God from our spirit so that it might water our mind. That wisdom is hidden for us, not from us. It is hidden in our spirit. When we pray in the Spirit, we are praying out and praying up those mysteries of God's wisdom He has deposited in our spirit at the new birth.

Many times when I need wisdom I pray in the Spirit. As I spend time praying in other tongues, inevitably wisdom will come to my mind on what is best to do. As I pray in the Spirit, the hidden mysteries of God's wisdom in my spirit are revealed to my mind. To access this wisdom requires us to live a life of dependence upon the Holy Spirit rather than leaning to our understanding or rationale.

One specific time, I needed wisdom about a twenty-acre piece of property our church owned. We had received a large offer for it, but the question the elders and I were praying about was whether it was the will of God to sell it or keep it to build on later. The elders asked me to come back to them with what I recommended since I had been the one who had located that property when we first purchased it several years before. I had been praying and had not heard anything specific on this.

I kept praying in the Spirit, and the day before we had to give an answer to the buyer, God's wisdom came to me. He let me know He had already placed the desire in my heart regarding this and He did not need to speak to me about this in any other way. His wisdom for me was He trusted me to follow the desire in my heart He had planted there. He also let me know this was the primary way He would lead me.

This was very liberating wisdom God gave me that day. We decided to sell the property, pay off our indebtedness on our youth building, sow into other ministries, and purchase another piece of property that would serve our vision that was much less than the property we sold. This wisdom and great outcome for our church all came by praying in the Spirit.

4. Praying in tongues builds up our faith.

> *But you, beloved, building yourselves up on your most holy faith, praying in the Holy Spirit* (Jude 20).

This is a very important and powerful benefit of praying in other tongues. The things we are in faith about come to us by hearing from God.

> *So then faith comes by hearing, and hearing by the Word of God* (Romans 10:17).

Once we hear from the Lord about a portion of His will and plan for our lives, we must respond to that and align ourselves with what He has said. The will of God is not automatic. When the devil gets wind of what we are doing from what we have heard from God, he will attempt to oppose us, discourage us, or distract us. Everything we hear from God has the potential of tearing down the devil's kingdom. So he will do all he can to stop us. The reality is, he cannot stop us unless we move our focus off what God has spoken to us and on people, circumstances, and problems he is using to hinder us.

Praying in the Spirit is helpful to keep our focus on the main things—on what God has said to us. Praying in tongues helps me to keep the main thing the main thing in my life. It helps to realign my thinking whenever my thoughts wander off what I have heard from God. It builds us up on our faith. Praying in tongues is very beneficial to staying in faith.

5. Praying in tongues keeps us in the love of God.

But you, beloved, building yourselves up on your most holy faith, praying in the Holy Spirit, keep yourselves in the love of God… (Jude 20-21).

Another great benefit of praying in tongues is it is helpful to keep us in the love of God. If we stay in faith and in love, we cannot be defeated. The enemy knows this. Therefore, he will do all he can to distract us with the carnality and immaturity of others, especially Christians. First Corinthians 13:8 tells us, *"Love never fails."* If we are experiencing failure in our lives it is usually a love failure.

And let's face it, the most difficult person to show love to is the sandpaper person in our lives. You know who I am talking about. That person who rubs you the wrong way. The one you have allowed to get under your skin. That person you have been praying to God to get out of your life. At the same time, the Lord is interceding at the right hand of the Father that you, "Allow Him to manifest through you into this person's life." You want the person out of your life and Jesus wants to get into his or her life through you!

You cannot fulfill this assignment of loving your sandpaper person unconditionally without His agape love flowing through you. It is true you have His love in you in your spirit. Yet speaking the Word and praying in other tongues will help release that love in you and keep you in the love of God with those not easy to love. I have discovered this to be true. As I pray in the Spirit, I am able to receive God's heart and perspective toward the person I am not happy with. Praying in tongues is very helpful to keep us in the love of God!

6. Praying in tongues helps us to draw on the Spirit and pray the perfect will of God.

> *Likewise the Spirit also helps in our weaknesses. For we do not know what we should pray for as we ought, but the Spirit Himself makes intercession for us with groanings which cannot be uttered. Now He who searches the hearts knows what the mind of the Spirit is, because He makes intercession for the saints according to the will of God* (Romans 8:26-27).

Have you ever been in a situation you did not know what or how to pray? I certainly have a number of times. This passage says the Holy Spirit will help us in those times of weakness, those times when we don't know the best way to pray. He makes intercession for us at those times through groanings and utterances that cannot be uttered with intelligible words.

The Greek word for "help" here means to take hold with another. The way the Spirit is going to help us is to take hold with us. This is a co-laboring kind of help He is offering to us. He is not going to do it for us without us! So when He speaks of making intercession for us, He is going to do this with us. He will use our groanings and our utterances that are unintelligible and cannot be understood—tongues.

I believe He will use our prayers in the Spirit, praying in other tongues to intercede through us and for us. And when He does, He is praying the perfect will of God on our behalf. In other words, praying in tongues is praying the perfect will of God because your mind and will are not involved at all. There is no opportunity for you to pray a selfish prayer when you pray in the Spirit. And the wonderful thing is the Holy Spirit will use your prayer in tongues to pray according to the will of God for your life. What a deal!

I have been praying in tongues at times when I did not know what or how to pray in English. As I spent time praying in the Spirit, the Holy Spirit let me know what I had been praying and then gave me the understanding to pray out in English. Praise God. This has happened so many times in my life it has become a habit with me now. I pray in tongues until I know what to pray with my understanding. This is what the Holy Spirit does through us when we pray in the Spirit. He helps our weakness of not knowing what to pray and He downloads to us the perfect prayer to pray with our understanding.

7. Praying in tongues will bring us into rest.

For with stammering lips and another tongue He will speak to this people, to whom He said, "This is the rest with which You may cause the weary to rest." And, "This is the refreshing"; yet they would not hear (Isaiah 28:11-12).

This is a clear declaration from God's Word that He will use tongues to bring us rest and refreshing. One thing that is obvious among God's people is that they need rest and refreshing. So many folks are full of anxiety, dread, and fear. This is not from the Lord. He told us in His Word to *"be anxious for nothing"* (Philippians 4:6). Then again He told us, *"Let not your heart be troubled"* (John 14:1). From my observation of the church, people are troubled and anxious about everything. There is no rest or peace in that state of mind.

My experience confirms this word from Isaiah. When I spend time praying in tongues, it causes me to draw on His rest, His peace, and His refreshing. It helps me keep my mind stayed on Him, trusting in Him instead of the whirlwind of circumstances around me. This brings me into perfect peace.

> *You will keep him in perfect peace, whose mind is stayed on You, because he trusts in You* (Isaiah 26:3).

In many places in the New Testament we see grace and peace connected: Romans 1:7, First Corinthians 1:3, Second Corinthians 1:2, and Galatians 1:3 are just a few of those references. What does this mean? Grace and peace go together like Greg and Janice and peas and carrots. It also means whenever we leave peace, we have left grace. That is not to condemn us. This is simply a barometer to help us monitor where we are spiritually. Praying in other tongues is one of the primary ways to keep our minds stayed on Him and bring us into a place of peace, rest, trust, and refreshing.

I have shared a number of benefits of praying in tongues with you. These benefits are nothing short of powerful and will position you to walk in the supernatural on a consistent basis. Many Christians sing that old hymn, "O, for a Thousand Tongues to Sing" and then they hear about one more tongue and act like this is heresy. No, this isn't heresy. It's the Word of God and it is a wonderful benefit of the Spirit-filled life we can all receive!

Chapter 21

DEVELOPING A PERSONAL RELATIONSHIP WITH THE HOLY SPIRIT

WHEN I GRADUATED FROM BIBLE COLLEGE, MY WIFE AND I planted our first church in Houston, Texas. We grew a lot in ministry experience in the three and one-half years we served there as pastors. One of the greatest lessons we learned was how important it was to depend upon the ministry of the Holy Spirit in both feeding people the Word of God and loving and caring for them.

When a new toll road caused the church building we were leasing to be condemned, we followed the leading of the Spirit and merged our church with another local church in the area.

After a time of praying in tongues and time in the Word, the Lord confirmed to us our next pastoral assignment would be in

North Texas. Because we had developed an intimate relationship with the Holy Spirit for many years by this time, His voice and direction became very clear to us. He is not confused about His will and the future He has planned for you and me. A little over a year later, we did in fact end up pastoring a great church in Decatur, Texas. We served as pastors of this life-giving church for twenty-four years.

Most of my key relationships today came as a result of our ministry in River of Life Church in Decatur, Texas. That is where I met Paul Milligan, the CEO of Andrew Wommack Ministries. That is where I met Andrew Wommack, as he was a guest speaker in my church for many years. And that is where I developed a relationship with my pastor, Bob Nichols, the pastor of Calvary Cathedral International in Ft. Worth, Texas. The Holy Spirit knows the plans He has for us! If we will value our personal relationship with Him, He will reveal all He has prepared for us.

> *But as it is written: "Eye has not seen, nor ear heard, nor have entered into the heart of man the things which God has prepared for those who love Him." **But God has revealed them to us through His Spirit...*** (1 Corinthians 2:9-10).

What a powerful passage of Scripture this is. The things God has prepared for us He reveals to us by His Spirit! Since that is true, it is imperative you and I purpose to develop an intimate, personal relationship with the Holy Spirit. The purpose of the final chapter of this book is to explain how any born-again Christian can have this kind of personal relationship with the Spirit. He really wants to reveal to us the great things God has prepared for us.

Developing a personal relationship with the Holy Spirit begins by receiving Jesus Christ as your Lord and Savior. You cannot know the Holy Spirit until you know Jesus as your Savior.

> *And I will pray the Father, and He will give you another Helper, that He may abide with you forever—the Spirit of truth, whom the world cannot receive...* (John 14:16-17).

The world cannot receive the Spirit without receiving Jesus as Lord. The second most important thing in having this kind of personal relationship with the Spirit is to receive the Baptism in the Spirit—to be filled with the Spirit. I shared about this in chapter 19 of this book. If you have not yet received the Baptism in the Spirit, you are not going to be as sensitive to His promptings and leading in your life. Typically, we follow what we are most full of. So many Christians are filled with knowledge from the world and follow the leading of their carnal minds or flesh. Though God loves us all the same, this type of Christian is not "tuned in" to the voice of the Spirit. Therefore, he or she does not receive all the good things He has prepared for each one.

The next thing that has helped me cultivate my relationship with the Holy Spirit is to pray in the Spirit—in other tongues—daily. I shared about this in chapter 20 of this book. Praying in the Spirit or praying in tongues develops our sensitivity to the leading of the Spirit in our life. The reason for this is when we are praying in other tongues it is our spirit that is praying. And the place the Holy Spirit resides in us is in our spirit.

> *But he who is joined to the Lord is one spirit with Him* (1 Corinthians 6:17).

If we are born again, our spirit is joined to His Spirit. Therefore, when we are praying in the Spirit, we are much more sensitive to the will of God because that is where He dwells. And it is in our spirit where He communicates with us. The more time we spend with Him, the more distinct and clear His voice and leading becomes to us. When my wife calls me on the phone, she doesn't say, "Hi Greg, this is Janice." She doesn't have to tell me her name. I know her voice. I could recognize her voice in a crowd of hundreds of people because I have spent time with her. I have spent the majority of my adult life with her and her voice is very distinct to me.

When you spend time with the Holy Spirit, His voice and leading will become just as clear and distinct to you as the voice of one of your close family members. The truth is, Jesus is present with us in the person of the Holy Spirit 24/7. The question is not whether He is present with us. The real question is, are we present to Him? Are we considering His presence, His will, His Word, and His heart on things in our decisions? I love the statement I heard Creflo Dollar say recently, "I choose to live in Your presence and walk in Your finished work!" That is so powerful and is my desire and choice to do daily as well.

Choose His Presence

We need the Holy Spirit in every area of our lives each day. We need Him in our marriages. We need Him in our relationship with our children. We need Him in our jobs. We need Him in our ministries. We need Him in our finances. We need Him involved with our physical bodies and our health. We need Him in our decision making. We need Him to help us understand the Word. We need Him in our witness to the world. We need Him in everything. We truly need Him every moment and every hour of every day!

There is not one area of our lives or one day of our lives we do not need the Helper, the Holy Spirit and His ministry to us. Without Him we can do nothing. Thank God we are not without Him! The question is, are we making our minds and hearts present to Him on a daily basis? The Holy Spirit is always available to speak to us and lead us. The real issue is, are we available to Him and present to Him more than our circumstances, people, and the natural reasoning of our minds? This is essential if we are going to develop a personal relationship with the Holy Spirit.

My wife and I have counseled literally hundreds, probably thousands, of people over the past four decades since we have been filled with the Spirit. One of the most important lessons we have learned in helping people is no two people or couples are the same. They may be dealing with the same problem, but the answer is not the same because of what is going on in the hearts of each individual. It takes the ministry of the Holy Spirit to show us which principle from the Word applies to each person or couple in each situation.

In the churches I pastored, I trained our leaders to help me counsel people who had problems in every area of life. I taught them to use the Word and depend on the Spirit. I also made sure they were clear about one thing: never assume you know the answer to the root problem in their lives without first listening to them and listening closely to the Holy Spirit. I would train my leaders by having them sit in with me with two or three individuals or couples who were requesting answers for their problems from the Word. By the third time, I would allow them to lead the individual or couple and I would observe. Then I would have them launch out on their own in their journey of discipleship of others.

In one case, a staff member, Donald, I had trained met with a couple who were considering separation in their marriage. I had to leave for an important family event and asked Donald to go solo with this couple, Larry and Rhonda. When they came in to meet with Donald, he asked each of them to share with him what they thought the root problem was in their marriage. Rhonda began by pouring her heart out complaining about Larry for twenty minutes without hardly taking a breath. She was talking and could not shut up, according to Donald. While she was talking and complaining, Larry sat in his chair with a smug look on his face. It was clear to Donald he was thinking, "See what I have to deal with all the time. I can't get a word in edgewise."

Donald listened to Rhonda and listened to Larry's body language through his arms folded and the smug look on his face. He also was praying quietly under his breath in the Spirit and listening to the Holy Spirit. After twenty minutes, Donald spoke out what He heard the Spirit say to him, "Larry, you are the problem in this marriage. You have failed to pay attention to your wife and minister to her emotionally. You have failed to take responsibility to cover your wife with prayer and give her unconditional love. And you are hiding behind her weaknesses to excuse your own!"

Larry was shocked and Rhonda immediately stopped talking with her mouth and eyes wide open. Larry was a good man who immediately repented to God and to his wife. He got down on his knees and wept while he apologized to her. The presence of God filled the room and this couple left with complete freedom and healing in their marriage. This all happened because Donald had developed a personal relationship with the Holy Spirit. He also had followed my instruction to depend on the Spirit to show him what the real heart issues and root problem is in the individual or couple before he attempted to give them an answer from the Word.

Larry and Rhonda both became true disciples of Jesus through Donald and his wife mentoring them after that time in his office. Thank God for the Holy Spirit! He knows everything about everyone and will help us help people if we will just listen to Him and follow His promptings.

> *But the Helper, the Holy Spirit, whom the Father will send in My name, He will teach you all things, and bring to your remembrance all things that I said to you* (John 14:26).

We need the Holy Spirit to teach us about everything that is important in our lives and is part of God's plan for our lives. Jesus was filled with the Spirit, led by the Spirit, and followed the Spirit throughout His life and ministry. If He needed the Holy Spirit, then we need the Holy Spirit. The Spirit, our Helper, will help us if we depend on Him and look to Him. No matter how many marriage books you have read by famous authors or parenting books you have read by Dr. James Dobson, you still need the Holy Spirit. He knows your spouse and your child better than you do. He will show you how to minister to them and love them if you will listen to Him and develop a personal relationship with Him.

"It's Your Fault"

A number of years ago our son Michael had done something he knew was wrong. He had clearly crossed a boundary my wife and I had set for him, and I was going to have to make sure he experienced some consequence for his decision to disobey us. He was seven years of age at the time and I sent him to my room and asked him to lean over the bed. I was about to apply the rod of correction to the seat of instruction for his bad decision. As I began to raise my hand holding the small dowel rod and apply it to Michael, I heard the Holy Spirit say, "It's your fault."

I stopped and told the Spirit quietly under my breath, "What do You mean, my fault? We told Michael if he did this he would get a spanking. He clearly violated what we said, rebelled against our word, and he needs to receive correction so he knows this boundary is serious with us and to him." I then started to raise the rod in my hand again and I heard the Spirit say almost audibly in my spirit, "I said it's your fault!" I told Michael to wait there for me for a couple of minutes, and I went into another room to pray. I think the waiting was harder on Michael than the spanking I hadn't been able to give him yet.

I went into another room and asked the Lord, "What did You mean when You said this was my fault? How were Michael's actions my fault?" He responded immediately and said, "Michael would rather receive negative attention than no attention at all. You haven't been spending intentional time with him and that's the reason he did what he did—to get your attention." Wow! I was stunned by this revelation of my oversight in my relationship with my son.

I went back into the bedroom, repented to Michael for my failure to spend quality time with him, and asked him to forgive me. He jumped in my arms and we had a great time of restoration. All because of a personal relationship with the Holy Spirit.

The Holy Spirit will help you with your marriage, with your children, your finances, your job, and your ministry. He will also help you to deal with heart issues in your own life. He is a life saver!

Obedience and Responsiveness

One final principle that has helped me develop a personal relationship with the Holy Spirit is instant obedience and responsiveness to His promptings in my heart. When I am sensing He wants me to give something to someone or to a particular ministry, I have conditioned myself to do it promptly. When I sense Him prompting me to call someone and encourage them, I do it as quickly as possible. When I feel Him leading me to stop and pray for someone, I do it right then, instead of just telling them I will be praying for them. When I hear Him tell me to give a word to someone, I just step out and do it.

I am not saying I do this perfectly every time. I have simply purposed in my heart to be a responsive and prompt follower of His leading in my life. This has caused me to develop sensitivity to Him and has increased my intimacy with Him. Most of the time I have experienced Him leading me to do something, it is very low risk to follow through. Whether it is by giving, praying for someone, encouraging someone, or giving someone a word from the Lord, there is very little risk involved.

I have learned to just step out and act on whatever inward prompting He gives me. And the results have been phenomenal. Healings, encouragement to others, signs, wonders, and miracles are the fruit of following His promptings. After a period of time I had many spiritual experiences I could use to compare to His present promptings and leading in my life. This makes following Him even easier.

> *These things we also speak, not in words which man's wisdom teaches but which the Holy Spirit teaches, comparing spiritual things with spiritual* (1 Corinthians 2:13).

Once you commit to follow His leading promptly in your life, you will begin to amass a storehouse of testimonies of how God used you in supernatural ways. You will also have many spiritual experiences that line up with His Word that you will be able to compare to any present prompting or leading you are sensing from the Spirit. This will produce tremendous confidence in you in hearing and following Him now and in the future.

Living Supernaturally

During the interview by the elders of the church in Decatur, Texas, they asked what my perspective was regarding the role of the pastor. I responded to them, "The pastor's role is to feed the people, love the people, and lead the people. And the only way I know how to pastor successfully is to pastor supernaturally. In other words, I will depend on the Spirit and listen to the Spirit in how to feed, love, and lead the people." That seemed to bless them and that is how I served the leaders and people there for twenty-four years and it bore much fruit.

The only way I know how to be a good husband to my wife is supernaturally. The only way I know how to be a good father to my four children and good grandfather to my eleven grandchildren is supernaturally. The only way I know how to serve in my present role as Director of Charis Bible College is supernaturally. The only way I know what to teach and how to minister effectively to others is supernaturally. I have a personal relationship with the Holy Spirit, depending on Him, listening to Him, and following Him daily. This is the only way to live inside His grace. After all, He is the Spirit of grace (Hebrews 10:29).

You can have a personal relationship with the Holy Spirit and live a supernatural life. It's not difficult. If I could find this and walk in it, you can. It doesn't come by making vows or through the strength of your will. It comes by trusting in Him, depending on Him, listening to Him, and following His leading in your life. This supernatural life and ministry is available to you right now. He is offering this new way of living, loving, and ministering to you today. I speak a word of release to you to trust the Spirit fully with your family, your finances, your career, your ministry, and your very life.

I speak courage to you as you step out in the release of the gifts of the Spirit through your life. I speak exciting kingdom adventures over you as you walk into the future God has planned for you. And I speak divine connections and divine appointments in your relationships. The supernatural will begin to flow through you in brand-new ways. Healings, miracles, signs and wonders will follow you. New pages in Acts chapter 29 will be written by you. You are destined for greatness. The best is yet to come in your life! Welcome into this amazing, supernatural life.

About the Author

Greg Mohr is the Director of Charis Bible College in Woodland Park, Colorado. He is also a conference speaker and author and served as Senior Pastor of River of Life Church in Decatur, Texas, for twenty-four years. He is a graduate of Rhema Bible Training Center in Broken Arrow, Oklahoma, and earned a Master's degree in Leadership from Southwestern Christian University in Bethany, Oklahoma. Greg is married to his best friend, Janice. Together they have four children and eleven grandchildren.

ALSO BY GREG MOHR

Your Healing Door